Path of a Prophet

Understanding the Journey

John Mark Pool

Path of a Prophet

Understanding the Journey

DESTINY IMAGE® PUBLISHERS, INC.

P.O. Box 310, Shippensburg, PA 17257-0310

"Speaking to the Purposes of God for this Generation and for the Generations to Come."

This book and all other Destiny Image, Revival Press, Mercy Place, Fresh Bread, Destiny Image Fiction, and Treasure House books are available at Christian bookstores and distributors worldwide.

For a U.S. bookstore nearest you, call 1-800-722-6774.
For more information on foreign distributors, call 717-532-3040.
Or reach us on the Internet: www.destinyimage.com

ISBN 13: 978-0-7684-2442-3

For Worldwide Distribution, Printed in the U.S.A.
1 2 3 4 5 6 7 8 9 10 11 / 09 08 07

Dedication

I dedicate this book to the most important spiritual influences of my life:

My wife-Sandy Montgomery Pool and my mom-Loriece Pool, without your love, devotion and prayers I could not have been here to complete the Father's will. Thank you for your true love.

Endorsement

I got interested in John Mark Pool when I saw his Prophesies come to pass. The bygone was the flooding of New Orleans. Then I interviewed him for TV and radio and got to know him better. But our bonding really took place on our trip to Israel. I saw his heart for people and especially for the Jewish people. His life and Israel have a great deal in common. Israel is in a crucible in preparation to become prophets and priests. No matter how far Israel fell God never gave up on His old covenant people. John Mark Pool has also been in the crucible of preparation. He is coming out of this training refined for end time ministry. As you read his story the anointing of end time ministry will drip off on you. Just as the Jew needs the Christian, you need this vital end time prophetic impartation. Enjoy, grow and go.

Shalom and Love

Sid Roth
President, Messianic Vision

Contents

Foreword

I wish it were instant, but it is not. There are no short cuts to becoming a prophet. Gifts are given, but character to carry the gift is forged in the fire of affliction. Believe me, I know!

Once I was asked the difference between prophetic ministry and a prophet. I said something like, "About twenty years!" I think you get the picture. We are each uniquely called, go through various stages of training; and then we are commissioned. It was that way with Moses, Elijah, and Elisha; and it will be that way with you.

You see, true prophets *become* a word—they don't just *give* a word. It is not enough just to receive a gift by grace (though that is awesome and incredibly fun) and release or deliver a word. Again, that is amazing, impacting, and life-changing to both the one who receives and the one who gives. But there is another level. You become a word! This process is called *incarnation Christianity*.

Now do not misunderstand me; Jesus is the only one who was in the bosom of the Father, took on flesh, and became the Word of God incarnate, as the first chapter of the Gospel of John so beautifully depicts. But in similar fashion, a true prophet does more than just dispense revelation—a true prophet becomes a word! This process takes time.

This process of becoming is a road less traveled. Many have been invited to step aside from the crowded path of instant fame and choose to pick up their cross and die daily.

One time I heard a very well known prophetic leader publicly state before a group of thousands, "I have the gift of rude." Perhaps the person was kidding. Perhaps this was a way of making excuses for inappropriate behavior. Maybe the speaker was having a difficult day. But the Jesus I know is the one who said kind things such as, *"If you want to be first in the Kingdom, learn to be the servant of all"* and *"The world will know that you are My disciples by the love you have one for another."*

His examples of servanthood tell us that the higher up you go in authority, the lower you must go in humility. Faith works through the channel of love. Increased authority comes from increasing your love. Love God. Love people. Love yourself! Increased revelation comes through increased worship! A voice that can be heard is one that has leaned itself on the chest of another and echoes the sounds of Heaven in earth. You must be in tune with the higher order—Jesus Christ!

Do you want to be a prophet used by the Lord to touch lives and impact nations? Then go on a journey with me, John Mark Pool, and others who have decided to live the life—those who daily pick up their crosses and follow Jesus to become what He destined for us.

With great joy, I commend to you the pages in your hand composed from the trenches along the path. Jesus took the bread and broke it saying, "This is my body, take and eat." In this book the author tears off pages of his life and invites you to experience the Path of a Prophet. You will benefit greatly from the testimony of a life laid down and the wisdom learned along the way.

Blessings to each of you,

James W. Goll
Cofounder of Encounters Network
Author of *The Seer, Dream Language,*
The Prophetic Intercessor and others

Preface

People want to know what is ahead of them, and many turn to various sources to try to get future information before it happens. People have been searching for a way to know the future since the beginning of their existence.

Millions of people on earth, both Christians and non-Christians alike, possess an inquisitive nature, wanting to know beforehand about the next curve in life. The inner workings of humans were designed with a yearning for something more—something more than we can fulfill ourselves.

For me, understanding things before they took place has been a way of life ever since birth. I will always remember my youthful days on our farm in Texas and seeing many strange occurrences. An *adventure* is one good way to describe this journey that God has allowed my life to explore. Although I was raised in a God-fearing home, that did not prepare me for the journey ahead.

When I was a youngster, I would never have guessed that my future path in life would lead me to such sorrowful and unknown places. Sitting here now as I write, recalling many such events, I would rather delete some of these chronicles. But, life is full of astonishing events—even for those reared in the strictest religious environments. Each of our journeys has many unforeseen predicaments that shape us into the person God wants us to become.

Every person is in the process of living life—each of us face multiple trials that open opportunities to embrace, or reject, the lessons of the Creator. In all His infinite wisdom, our heavenly Father decided to give us choices. We can learn from all the kings and kingdoms that have risen and fallen and serve to formulate a helpful map, or we can make the same mistakes as the dusty trail leads us on.

Pause and consider the path you and I travel through life. This trip is not merely the result of Big Daddy God enjoying a great laugh over our trials and tribulations. Not at all! It is the essence of our existence; our explorations shape our spirits that are searching to fulfill the desire deposited in us by God. Our caring Father formed each of us uniquely with a strand of spiritual DNA. Our journey will bring forth transformations of our inner person. However, because we are free to make choices, as my life clearly demonstrates, some of our choices take us the long way around to reaching His goals for us.

God gave life to man and woman just as He declared in His Word. Yet we have to die to ourselves along the journey of life in order to begin to understand an earth with a Kingdom perspective. Literally and physically dying dramatically changed my view of life along the path to becoming. Simply knowing that God cares so much about me that He sent His only Son down a long road to save me from being eternally lost made me realize how much He loves me—and you.

Yes, Jesus has traveled where every person has gone before—and then some! Jesus walked on the shores of the Sea of Galilee and ate fish with the common people of His day. He does not ask us to leave our paths before our adventures are finished here on earth; because He hopes that through every obstacle and around every blockade, we will begin to see that all of the low places and flooded highways were not the disasters we thought, if they turned our hearts toward Him.

Many of us learn early on that the safest way to travel our life path is down the middle of the lane designed for us. Many have learned to travel while maintaining a safe speed and driving between the lines of established highways; but the adventurous and the pioneering spirit seem to be the foundation for those called to hear His voice and speak His words. If we pay enough attention to embrace the path, we will hear His voice as signposts along our way.

I have discovered that God has a very interesting process for those of us who know we are the bearers of the news that is just over the next mountain. He brings us down the road of resurrection decisions, and as we make proper choices, the extra equipment we thought was so valuable loses its luster. His people, who adjust to becoming intimately hungry for Him in this process, find that showing others the right direction on their adventure becomes exhilarating.

Yes, Daddy sure has a way of shaping His signposts and buglers! The road I have been compelled to journey is much like an endless endurance trail rather than a path. No, actually it has been closer to a demolition derby! Keep your compass close by as you read so as not to take the same wrong roads.

Sometimes the path that molds us must be the very journey that breaks us! Keep your eye on achieving God's desire for you and off of the potholes in the road, and you will enjoy your life's safari. At times the path has a way of crushing human desire in exchange for His voice. Be encouraged with the road on which God has you. If you are not sure about which way your path is going, then I hope my story, as well as thousands of other voices of God, help you find your direction.

God gave me all the necessary equipment early on the road, and for a while it was as smooth as a traffic-free, eight-lane expressway. However, somewhere in the middle of a traffic jam, I lost the compass, the map, and the ability to see past the nose on my face! When you take detours, cannot read the road signs, and have a sense that you are going too far on an unmarked road, you could be in for a big surprise!

The *Path of a Prophet* does not offer you a glamorous adventure—I wish it did. Rather, it offers you evidence that the journey is full of twists, turns, and misguided directions. Sometimes we are given a map by others that only works for them, leading us on dark side trips lasting years with fears of never finding home. Hopefully the path described in my life's journey offers enough real-life, side-trip experiences that your adventure will be made much easier—learning from my trails and trials.

The enemy does not want us to finish the course of God's mission. Yet I would venture to guess that all the prophets of old would desire to be on the very path we are exploring today. I believe they knew, as many of us who have survived a few crashes understand, that the best is just over the next ridge. If you want to know the secrets that lie ahead for your life in this exciting voyage, then you need to follow the *Path of a Prophet* to point you in the right direction.

This is your time—God placed you here now. Heaven and earth will pass away, but His Word will never leave you. If you embrace this path, your adventure will help return the hearts of His children back to the Father.

The path of a prophet is the mantle that molds the Father's servants into a clear and accurate company of voices the world is yearning to hear.

CHAPTER I

Dirt Road to Heaven

"Auntie-n-Unkie from Okie Homie comes ta see us t'day!" I told my mother one day when I was three years old. According to Mom's account, she asked me to repeat what I said. Upon hearing the same sentence twice from a little toddler, she said she had a "knowing down in her spirit person" that God was giving her a "heads up" about what was soon to take place. Since she walked closely with God and was quite accustomed to hearing His voice on a 24/7 basis, she explained that the Holy Spirit's witness of urgency came up within her to begin cleaning and cooking in preparation for guests.

At three years old, I had never seen or visited any of our relatives from Oklahoma. It might as well have been Mars or Acapulco to my infant knowledge level. In the early '50s, we had a telephone but not all folks did, especially in the rural Texas farmlands. Therefore, much of the communication came through Western Union cables, cards, letters, and word of mouth passed along by acquaintances. (When Mom said, "We got word that..." it usually meant someone told someone who in turn told someone else....) In consideration of the day and the lack of regular communication channels, it was not uncommon for relatives and friends to simply show up on your doorstep announcing they had come to "visit awhile." And "awhile" could mean a *long* while.

Needless to say, my aunt and uncle showed up that day. Mother was always amused when she recounted that first prophetic word I spoke as a child. She pointed back to that day as God affirming His prophetic ministry mantle, activated by an undeniable confirmation.

Heritage and Home

"Son, you have no choice but to do the will of God," Mother emphasized. Understanding Mom Pool will give credence to that statement. Lula Loriece (Lane) Pool was born in Soper, Oklahoma, to poor dirt farmers, and was very familiar with the voice of God. She accompanied her father, Alexander Campbell Lane, on evangelistic trips around the rural regions of Central and Southern Oklahoma. They traveled by buckboard wagon setting up "brush arbors" as he preached uncompromising truths of God's Word and the power of the Holy Ghost evidenced by speaking in other tongues just as the Lord displayed in Acts 2:4. She told of many conversions to Jesus by entire families, and most were immediately filled with the Baptism of the Holy Ghost as they began to speak in other tongues. She told me the history of my family heritage, especially the days when revival fire broke out across the state and region, and many were miraculously healed of every form of disease.

When I responded to a major decision in my life by surrendering to the "call of God to preach the Gospel" at 12 years of age, Mother sat me down one day and told me a story that has never left my spirit.

"Son," Mother recalled, "you were still in my womb as I was expecting your birth when the Lord drew me in very close to Him and began to speak to me about you. Son, I had been fasting as much as I could while carrying you and praying to the Lord about what you were to be for this world. As I knelt by the sofa in our farmhouse living room, I was crying out to the Lord for a word about you when I distinctly heard His reply: 'His Name will be Mark and he will be my voice to the nations!'"

Mom told me that she looked up and around the room and no form of anyone was present. She told me it was a "spiritual hearing," and then with open eyes and mind she heard it once again, crystal clear and in a very loud, audible voice, *"His name will be Mark and he will be my voice to the nations!"* She said those are the only two times that she experienced the audible voice of God.

As Mother continued to share this treasured moment with me, she emphasized the fact that she withheld this revelation from me until then so as not to sway what the Holy Spirit would do if allowed to confirm His way in my life's calling. I appreciate that she waited to tell me, so we knew without a shadow of doubt that only God spoke and only He confirmed the words His way at His time. This is a very good example for parents to obey for their children's directions from God in their destiny.

After her story was finished, I began to cry, and she held me close. This is one of the most treasured memories I hold dear to my heart to this day. Mom went to be with the Lord in March 2002, having full knowledge that her words from God were being fulfilled as she passed into His glorious presence. I will never forget her last words to me, "Son, tell me, is it true that you are obeying the Lord in full-time preaching and ministering His words to the world?" I resolutely reassured her that God was keeping me busily engaged in full-time ministry.

I was talking with her on the church phone in my ministry office at the time, and I shared the works that God was performing through the prophetic words that He was pouring through me day after day to hungry hearts ready for the "now word" to transform their lives. I thought of the day John the Baptist sent his disciples to Jesus to ask Him if He is really the Messiah or did they need to look for another. I have a softer view of this Scripture passage, having been unable to be with Mom as she passed into God's glory.

I visualize now why John may have asked his question— simply to hear a reassuring reply from His Jesus, the man he baptized and who would soon be killed for speaking the truth boldly and without reserve. We cannot judge John for his question until we are in the dungeon about to lose our heads because of an earth-transforming revelation ripping into all religious veneer and exposing the enemy of our eternal completion. John lost his life completing his assignment—actions speak louder than words!

I pondered these thoughts concerning my dying mother's question, and heard myself saying, *"The blind see and the lame walk; the lepers are cleansed and the deaf hear; the dead are raised up and the poor have the gospel preached to them"* (Matt. 11:5 NKJV). I heard her sigh with a contentment that seemed to please her soul. I had no idea that those words would be our last this side of Heaven. Nonetheless, I have a peaceful resolve knowing she had peace in her spirit as she released it unto our Lord Jesus.

A lot has occurred since I surrendered my life to preach the Gospel by walking that pine floor aisle of our small East Texas country "full Gospel" church at the age of 12. I received the Lord as my Savior at the age of 7 in the living room of our farmhouse, repeating a prayer from Mom while we knelt in front of that same sofa she knelt in front of when hearing my name called out by God. Back in those days, our furniture outlasted many a person who sat on it!

I remember unloading of all those "heavy sins" from my shoulders that day, such as telling over-glamorized stories of major battles fought around the farm with my toy cap pistols and my "Red Ryder" outfit—single-handedly settling major Indian uprisings. You know the sins that come with 7-year-olds—pinching your older sister, chewing gum, and laughing out loud at jokes and pokes on the church pews.

God and Dad had a keen way of working together to quell such "sinners," and being instantly transplanted by the hand of the Almighty via my father into the pew immediately in front of him seemed to work very effectively. I will never forget the day we boys could not stop laughing until the right hand knuckle of justice came down firmly on our topknots to reassure us we were closer to judgment than we knew!

Those days are still fond memories of how church attendance and attention were never optional. I believe one of the main reasons I am still here today is because of my parents' faithfulness. Later processing cannot take away the early raising—remember that when raising your children. It is not an option before God whether or not to train up your child in the ways of the Lord (see Prov. 22:6). However you were raised, learn to keep only the "sweet" that God gives us. For example, I remember some church songs that we sang had no real scriptural basis. I really do not want a little cabin in the corner of Heaven! Instead, I want all of God with everything He has for me along the path. I do not want to miss anything I am supposed to do along the way; I just want to please Him and be His voice, saying everything I am supposed to say.

<h2 style="text-align:center">Boomers and Bloomers</h2>

Being born in 1952, a textbook baby boomer, I have observed and participated in the communications technology transformation that has revolutionized our world. From having no television in our home to having them in cars and in wireless handheld devices, this is a different world of communications from the one even our parents knew. Computer technology has made the globe grow incredibly smaller nearly overnight. Only 30 years ago it took weeks for me to receive letters from home while living in Africa as a resident foreign missionary. I can still remember going to the post office and to the cable desk to send a "wire" to people who needed to be reached quickly! Now we have "instant messaging," satellite communications, and high-speed Internet connections—all developed within a very short period of time.

As I look back on that childhood experience of delivering my first prophetic word to my mom, it reminds me of one of God's basic principles for communicating through His messengers—keep a "childlike" faith.

Peering over my shoulder now, I smile as I often use this illustration while teaching in prophetic schools: "You cannot be too smart to be a prophetic voice for God. If you are a very analytically minded person, you will have problems because bringing forth a prophetic word cannot come from your mind. It must come from God's mind to your heart and through you as a conduit to His people!"

It is as if I can still hear Mother talking to me at times. Those developmental days were extremely foundational for beginning the process of the prophetic mantle. During those times there were both good and not-so-good experiences. I have since learned and have said many times, "You have to be born and raised somewhere, and you have to learn to take the good and spit out the rest!"

I wanted the next step after salvation, the Baptism of the Holy Spirit, more than I wanted my next breath. I did what everyone in those days was supposed to do—I sought it. If you were known to "seek the baptism," then you could be assured that every altar call you responded to was going to be an experience. We had two long, varnished-but-worn, 2-by-12s joined side-by-side making our "men's" altar roughly 24 inches by 16 feet long. The same spanned the opposite side for the women. As a young "seeker" I had many helpers. All I had to do was get on my knees at the altar and the helpers for God would make sure that I did not go away empty. Many meant well, but the overdose of help caused me at times to do a "courtesy drop" or just fall out in the spirit, mostly the "spirit of exhaustion!" That was church when I was a youngster.

In those days, you just had to seek. It was not understood that you could just believe, expect the Holy Spirit to fill you, and simply begin speaking in a heavenly language. It was real work back then. People gathered around and coached me. "Just let go and speak out, son!" "There it is, son, it is right in your throat." Then they would grab my jaws and move them up and down to help God!

I was one worn-out seeker when an evangelist came to our church to hold a revival. I don't know why this meeting was so different, but the Holy Spirit really began to move. The evangelist,

Brother "Red River" Jordan, they called him, pointed to me in the front row and said, "Young man, the Lord told me you were hungry for the Baptism of the Holy Ghost. Is that true?" I ran down to the front without as much as a word just nodding my head "yes" and knowing that I was about to be overfilled with the Baptism of the Holy Ghost. He simply laid his hands on my head and said, "Receive it now, in the Name of Jesus." Did I ever receive it! I understand now that the evangelist had prophetic gifts and simply had a "call out word." Because of my prophetic calling, the ignition of the Holy Spirit came about as a result of faith activated by obedience when the word was given.

They told me about the meeting the next day. Mom said they carried me out to our 1955 Plymouth station wagon, laid me in the back, and I didn't stop speaking in my heavenly language even as I drifted off to sleep that night in my bed. Yes, everything I have ever done has been just like that—with great gusto! I believe firmly that God has to make things unmistakably clear for some of us so we will not doubt it away later.

Many times during the process of becoming, the enemy tried to steal God's deposits, but it never once worked. I could not deny that the power of God and His Holy Spirit are as real as the ink on this page!

Just prior to my teen years, God had moved us from the farm into town. We attended the First Full Gospel Denominational Church and had access to more international speakers. During that period, I was feeling an intensity of the calling of God on my life. It seemed as if we were in church every other day during that time. God's calling has always been strong, but understanding how I was supposed to respond was very difficult, especially with the knowledge and training I had about building the Kingdom of God. God led me through some very difficult doors so I could see for myself that some men's view of "doing church" is extremely different when compared with God's Kingdom come on earth as it is in Heaven.

During this time the enemy made his first of several attempts to steal my life. I fell about 20 feet out of a tree near our new home. I landed on my back, and my head was only inches away from the exposed spiral blade of a push lawn mower. Mom noticed something wrong and took me to the emergency room. She described my inexplicable reaction to the shock from the fall. On the way to the hospital, mom said that I cried out loud in a stream of prayer that went directly into praying in the Holy Spirit's heavenly language. At the hospital, I was diagnosed as having a concussion.

Many times since that day the enemy has made attempts to take my life. This is one of the least attractive ingredients that accompany many on this prophetic pathway. Dying is just part of living in the journey for God's prophetic adventure.

As a youth, I was an avid lover of the Lord and wanted so much to do what He had called me to do. As leader of my Christ Ambassador's youth group, I was asked to preach during youth-led services at our church. One very memorable experience taught me the price of "the call" versus "the sway" of the present world to draw me along a downward path. I was scheduled to preach on the Sunday following the high school prom. I had never been to a prom, but wanted to go to one before I graduated from high school.

A very sweet and "straight-laced" young Jewish girl invited me to go with her to the prom. The invitation touched my heart, and I knew this was a major ordeal for her to step out of her comfort zone and ask me to be her date. I accepted out of a desire to be gracious to her as a friend, and because Pentecostals and Jews were very much looked upon in those days as "different" from the region's majority Southern Baptists. I knew this was a tough thing for her to do, and I also wanted to go to a youth dance. I was not allowed to attend dances, and there were no alternatives to have fun; we were taught only "thou shalt not!" In an act of rebellion, I accepted her invitation but kept it very low key. I did not necessarily try to hide it, but I didn't want to advertise it to the "full-Gospel church folk" either.

We had a wonderful evening, all under the watchful eyes of many chaperones. I even enjoyed innocently dancing to a couple of songs. The dancing was fast, similar to the jitterbug style, so my friend and I never as much as touched each other. However, why God placed a photo on the front page of the local newspaper of us dancing still puzzles me! Yes, there I was, revealed in all my indiscretion, dancing with a very attractive Jewish girl. The article was celebrating the way the students were enjoying the great gala with such diversity!

I might as well have been dressed in a red suit with cape and red pitchfork, according to the church leaders! I was chastened from the pulpit and asked to walk through repentance and restitution, vowing never again to go outside the faith and rules of the church to commit such horrible sins. I agreed but felt totally defeated, unable to tell my side of the story. God had a way of healing me, but the sting burned into my memory and reappeared in my future.

Called Out

Not long afterward, our church had a special guest speaker, a missionary from Africa, and all I could do for days was dream about the "Dark Continent" and the souls being lost without the knowledge of Jesus Christ as their Savior. I cried when I thought about what he said. Then the missionary asked those who felt the call of God to the foreign mission field to come forward and surrender their lives to the calling. I was sitting midway back in the middle of our large youth group; the next thing I knew, I was walking down the aisle to the front as if on air.

The missionary was a big man, and he had some of the biggest hands and feet I had ever seen. He grabbed me and prayed over me, and I began to bawl like a baby. Finally I felt the burden lift that had been weighing on me for so many days prior. I fell out in the spirit and immediately saw hundreds of Africans around me; and I was sharing the Gospel message with them. That vision was warmth to my soul. Little did I realize then how much of a reality God's words over me would later become.

With the call of God so strongly on my life, I felt the world was in front of me. All I had to do was go out and preach the Word and all would come to know Him. Little did I realize that this would be the revelation that helped me pass through many a fiery furnace along the path. Much like salvation, the calling of God for His purpose in your life is the beginning of the long road to qualification of that gift. Qualification is a very long and arduous journey indeed! *"For the gifts and the calling of God are irrevocable"* (Rom. 11:29 NKJV). That means those who are called of God, as in His fivefold leadership anointing, will be held to a more responsible level of judgment.

Many who receive this calling would abandon it unless "irrevocably" called, for it provides the utmost proving of the servant whom He has called to bring about the qualifying process. This in no way says the mouth is more important than the foot, etc., but rather it holds that accountability to a more stringent gauge than in others. This proving process is done for the sake of the whole Body of Christ so that the saints will not receive wolves in sheep's clothing.

If you have a call on your life as one of God's prophetic voices, write it down now in your Bible that it is not *if*, but *when* you go through the *"processing."* You will emerge as tried by fire and be as refined gold! Our refinement will benefit our Father's Kingdom that is now coming *"on earth as it is in Heaven."* God gives us a mantle and brings us to a gate with keys delivered by His own Son, paid for with a very high price. Yet, we may never use the key to unlock a gate that waits for our journey.

If we are obedient to follow that pathway to God, then the process, my comrade, in the Kingdom, is the very *process of your mantle from God to become tailored to His own voice. He who has ears to hear, let him hear what the voice of the Lord would say.* He speaks to those servants, His prophets, and this journey affords them processing for progressing in refinement to detect even a slight tone in the Father's small, still voice. This adventure to God is part of the process of becoming and it is never ever a duty.

In the 1970s when I was preparing to go into the mission field, I wore my hair just barely over the tops of my ears, as deemed the normal fashion of the day. (If today you saw a picture of what I looked like then, you would think I was a perfect example of how altar boys should dress for church!) In preparation for becoming a missionary, I was offered a pulpit at a little country church from a man who had known me for many years.

I arrived early, as was the custom when preaching in a new pulpit out of town. I met this man at the door of his little wooden rural "church in the sticks," and he took one look at me, whistled aloud, and said, "Wow! Oh my, John Mark! You sure have changed a lot since I saw you last—before you went off to that worldly college." I asked him if my weight loss was that noticeable. "No, it's not that," he said very sternly. Then he grabbed my hair at the edge of my ears and said, "Your hair length is unacceptable appearance for my pulpit. Therefore, I am going to ask you to understand that I will preach tonight. Contact me later if you get it cut according to our standards." He then turned and walked back into his office and shut the door.

I was appalled, flabbergasted, and speechless as I loaded the car and drove the long distance—with no money and no offering for missions—back to my home. One question that kept bouncing around in my head: Why did all the other church leaders where I preached accept me if my hair was not according to the standards? I cried out asking God to help that man, because he and his church were living as if holiness was something approachable, obtainable, or recognizable from the outside.

This experience helped me understand later why I chose paths least expected from where I had been. People want real true love that only the Father gives and is not based on an evaluation of your performance or appearance. Most members in the churches I visited back in those days knew very little about the Father's pure love. Love is about a relationship and not a demonstration to prove to others if you are "acceptable or unacceptable."

Wisdom is very important; however, please understand that no matter your level of education or formal training, it is not the "intelligence" of the person that makes him or her a qualified or seasoned prophetic voice for God. You must learn how *not* to depend on intelligence to release the words that God speaks to and through you. Embracing a "childlike faith" will help you become a person who hears from God. *Childlike* means to have the "innocence of a child," to disregard the negative and polluted system pumped into us early on which robs us of the innocent quality we need to be God's messengers.

Few children at the age of three have the mental capacity to naturally form complex sentences such as, "Auntie-n-Unkie from Okie Homie coming t'day!" That is why I believe there will be a major increase in the number of children who will be in the front row during the next wave of God's communication with His earth. We must have "childlike" faith simply to know that it is God speaking and that we should not add or take away any of His words, no matter how ridiculous they may sound to our "brilliant and mature" minds!

If we change what we hear to adjust to circumstances, people, feelings, geography, or any other seemingly "sound mental reasoning," then we have perhaps altered the entire meaning of what Jehovah God is speaking to a person, situation, region or nation! Just speak the word, and let God give further illumination from the Holy Spirit as to the purpose for the "cable from Heaven."

Prophets have a responsibility and may very well be required to "contend with a prophetic word" and be vigilant to see it brought about. Warring for the completion of the prophetic word is not an illustration that bypasses the sovereign hand of God, who will bring about His divine providence to fulfill an accurate prophetic word. During the process of becoming a prophet, you will learn about activating the prophetic gifts to see His words come to proper completion.

Meanwhile, Back on the Farm

Often we miss God's voice because we do not hear Him speak! I thank God that Mom was hearing and paying attention to a child's simple statement about an impending visit from relatives.

I thought about that seriously one day. Would I be attentive enough in my busy world to hear a 3-year-old child prophesy to me about something I needed to do to prepare for a sudden or unexpected turn of events? It helps to ponder those things in relation to the actual events you can recall in your own life.

Mom fondly told the story to me again before she graduated to her eternal reward with Jesus. She said that no sooner did she finish getting the house cleaned and dinner and other meals made ahead, than a car drove up the long dirt driveway toward the front porch where only a few hours earlier I had made my prophetic declaration. Sure enough, her family from Rush Springs, Oklahoma, just "appeared out of nowhere," as the Texans used to say.

Many from my former home state say, "All roads to Heaven go through Texas!" I did get to Heaven from Texas, and the journey has been very interesting. From the dirt trail on our farm to Heaven and back has been one exciting adventure after another!

I can still remember the day that running barefoot seemed as close to Heaven as a boy could imagine. I had all the fun a 7-year-old could ever want or desire right there on our modest rural farm. There were trees to climb, tree houses to build, and an infinite number of nooks and crannies to conquer. My earliest childhood memories of the Lord talking directly to me take place on the wide wooden porch of our farmhouse.

One day I was conquering the nearby woods down our long, dirt road a good distance from our home, when something behind the trees caught my eye. It seemed to be a figure or maybe a dark shadow. I became so frightened that I pretended that nothing was there. After I put some distance between me and whatever was following me, I mustered enough courage to glance over at the woods again. All of a sudden I felt deathly ill—short of breath and my heart felt as if it was going to explode inside my chest. I wasn't a sickly child; I was a typical healthy little boy.

Although I felt dizzy and my chest hurt, I ran home as fast as I could without passing out. I was afraid I was going to fall over dead. I had a fearful feeling that something was dreadfully wrong. I felt bad from the inside out—as if something evil was haunting me. I was panting and gasping for air as I ran into the house and fell down on the sofa and began to cry. Mom, immediately alarmed, picked me up and held me close to her. She carried me to the rocking chair and asked me what happened. After I explained, she prayed and rocked me.

Her prayers made me feel much better, and she asked if I was still feeling sick. I told her that my heart hurt—but it was not like any pain I had ever felt before. I didn't want to die and not know Jesus as she did. She smiled and said, "I think you need to kneel by the sofa and ask Jesus Christ to come into your heart. You need to know that you are His child—and that He loves you very much."

A "knowing witness" came up from within me, and I knew that what she said was true. I slid out of the rocker onto my knees, and on the bare wooden floor of the living room, with Mom's help, I repeated the prayer of salvation and received Jesus Christ into my heart. When parents encourage their children and guide them into the arms of the Lord, their children will have a solid foundation on which to stand when they reach out for answers to life's questions. Although as adults we choose whether or not to obey the Lord, we are most blessed if we had godly parents who instilled proper Christian foundations before life's storms began.

I still remember praying those words to ask Jesus Christ to come into my life and heart and forgive me of all my sins—such as calling my sister a "spoiled brat," taking an extra cookie, or chewing gum in Sunday school. When I said "amen," all the fear, pain, and the dark shadow following me instantly disappeared! Peace that passed all my understanding came over me in that moment of surrender. A thousand pounds lifted off my little shoulders, and I knew that I now belonged to Jesus and He belonged to me. What a day that was in our farmhouse at the end of the dirt road! Even though I was very young, I knew that the "shadow in the woods" was very real and if he got his way, I would die.

I remember that experience as if it happened yesterday. What is so unusual about that? A lot has happened to me since then; but as I traveled down different paths, failing to obey the signs, that moment on my knees in the living room never escaped my memory. I know that Jesus loves me—no matter what!

After you receive the unconditional love of the Lord in your life, you understand that whether or not the road you are on is dirt, gravel, or a major freeway, the ever-present "shadows of darkness" will never penetrate you. You *know* that the love of Jesus completely covers you from all of the enemy's attacks.

When you realize the power of the true love that Jesus offers you, that knowledge and understanding dispels all fear. I certainly did not have an advanced spiritual understanding at the age of seven, but I did not have any fear as I often walked by that same spot where I had felt the enemy's presence. My fear was gone because of my experience with God, and I wanted to know more about my new relationship with Jesus. After I confessed having Jesus Christ as my Lord, the darkness did not bother me. I was totally free from fear of the unknown.

It was wonderful having my newfound friend and "shepherd guide" as a close comfort as I merged from life's dirt trails onto the freeways. Life seems to go faster as you advance from dirt to pavement. My path has many fond memories; many include our Texas farm. I go by from time to time when in the Lone Star State—the memories now closer than the actual view. The dirt road is now paved, a symbol of advancement and improvement. Although we cannot remain stagnant in the past, we have to realize that the way we were raised has helped shape our future. Incorporate the best of the past and discard the rest. Develop wonderful dreams as you travel the new road God has placed before you, knowing His way is best!

Shortly after I asked Jesus into my heart, we moved from the farm to a suburban area of the state. We lived on the edge of the city limits, close enough to the woods to develop my outdoorsman abilities. Our family often reminisced about times past as we sat around the dinner table. My dad told us how he and his brothers had to hunt for food for the family during the winter on their farm. Their hunting was not for sport but for meat on the table. My fondest memories then and now are about life in rural Texas—the best years of my childhood growing-up days.

Homegrown Advice

During my process of becoming a prophet, I received much "homegrown advice"—from "wait upon the Lord" to "take the Gospel to the world now!" More and faster were the keys; and Jesus was always about to return, so I did not have time to lie prostrate on the floor for a few days and focus on Jesus. *Love* in those days was being thankful I was "saved" and/or "sanctified" (depending on the group's lingo), and that I was baptized in the Holy Ghost and fire—praising God that I was not going to hell.

If a person could love like that, attend church twice on Sunday and for sure on Wednesday nights, only then did he have real potential for becoming a church leader. You were not guaranteed to make it, but you had potential. For the next few years the leaders watched you, ensuring that you attended services enough times, shouted enough, spoke in tongues enough, hollered at prayer meetings enough, and talked like the other "totally sanctified" people.

Being raised in that type of judgmental environment where regular doses of the "fear and trembling of a terrible God" were dispensed, I felt as if I was living on the edge of losing it all. What if the much anticipated "rapture" took place and I was not standing within the strict and structured lines? I might be lost forever, and burned along with the condemned earth.

I thank God that He showed me His grace and mercy at home, which balanced the negativity at church during those years. He helped me realize that my God-fearing—but loving—Christian family placed the greatest value, not on rules and judgments but on instilling morals and ethics that would carry me through life in good standing. My "meat and potatoes" upbringing focused on the positive values of living honestly for God.

Although there were a lot of things about which I disagreed with our church leaders, there was a common foundation of *respect*—respect for the Lord, family, community, nation, and world. Sadly, it seems that the meaning of the word *respect* has been lost along the way between the dirt road and the paved expressway.

CHAPTER 2

The Journey

THE GOOD OLD DAYS?

When the old folks sat around the kitchen table in our farmhouse and talked about the "good old days," I remember thinking to myself, "I'll never talk like that when I get old!" Nonetheless, here I am doing just that—hoping to pass on helpful insights.

Although as a little boy I loved living on the farm, I found that growing up in suburban East Texas provided some of the best days of my life. Looking back and comparing other times, I realize that the '50s and '60s really were the "good old days."

We lived in a solid middle-class neighborhood—a great setting for raising a family. My dad, actually my stepfather, worked as a maintenance mechanic at a huge chemical plant that was then owned by Kodak (the large U.S. film and camera products corporation). Although Mom did not work outside the home, she worked hard taking care of five children, maintaining our home, and being a wife to Dad. Mom and Dad did everything they could to provide us with an enjoyable life. Most of the families in the neighborhood shared the same lifestyle, and the kids all became close friends. We had lots of good times together playing fun kid games outside—the harmless trouble we got into could fill a book. Fortunately Mom and Dad were not aware of most of our antics, unless one of the kids blabbed it to his parents and word got around quickly to the other parents. Those were the "dreaded days" we hoped would not last long.

In those days the public schools had teachers who thought of their profession more as a "calling" than a job, and the students and teachers treated each other with respect. We rode our bicycles to and from school each day, and when we got older we would ride our motorbikes. Almost every kid had a Honda. I started out, however, not on a Honda, but on a Sears and Roebuck motor scooter. I didn't care; I was just thrilled to have it to ride. I drove it mostly because I was two years older than Sam, my younger brother, and I had a paper route. Delivering papers justified the scooter, and having two routes helped pay for gas. I would let Sam help me with the smaller route.

I can still smell the paper and ink in the back pressroom coming off the press every evening. We "paper boys" would gang up in the distribution room planning fun for the coming weekend. Back then we listened to Elvis Presley, Ritchie Valens, Buddy Holly, and Chuck Berry. I remember when "The House of the Rising Sun" by the Animals was released—the radio played it over and over. Music was a big part of life for us, especially at the Friday night football receptions, the biggest events on earth in that day. Our group did not believe in dancing, but somehow I was able to get around it all. I wanted to be in the swing of things and have fun—just like most kids.

There were probably some kids who were using illegal drugs back then, but because of the crowd I ran with, I actually never saw marijuana until I was in college. The extent of our trouble-making consisted of the "bad guys" in our group sneaking cigarettes from their parents and pilfering a jug of some "rot-gut hooch." We told our parents we were "going camping," and then we would pass around the booze and smoke cigarettes. Camping was fun! Camping gave us an excuse to get away from home for the entire Friday night and most of Saturday. The house rules: as long as my grades were up, the homework and schools projects were done, and my room was somewhat clean, I could go camping with guys that my parents either knew personally or at least knew their parents.

Our "hooligan gang" was connected by paper routes, church, school, or the neighborhood, and could be found on any given weekend hunting for squirrels, rabbits, or anything small in season. When a few too many of us got together at the same time, then we usually ended up in trouble. Our antics included rolling and tossing toilet paper all over girls' yards, and the really "dirty" trick that involved cow manure. One of the guys would retrieve some extremely fresh manure and put it in a paper grocery bag. Then we would place the bag in front of the door of a girl's home, douse it with lighter fluid, and then light it while ringing the doorbell. We jumped on our bikes, sped out around the corner, then stopped to watch the dad try to stomp the manure fire out with his bare feet or slippers!

Eventually the bicycles were traded for motorcycles which was both a good and bad thing. Although we became very capable on them, we learned to be careful, especially after one of our friends rode his motorcycle into a parked flatbed tractor-tailor rig and was killed instantly. We had often ridden together, and I believe this was another time when God spared my life.

Mostly our weekends were filled with light chicanery. We were required to be a part of the "church scene" every week and were involved in youth group activities. Most of the time, we wanted to be decent kids just enjoying life. We had a few bad days, though, like the time Gary decided to make homemade blackberry wine. The smell was bad, but the results of drinking it were much worse.

Another time, Gary and I rode our bikes downtown about 2 A.M. to lob off a couple of "cherry bombs" as close to the police station as possible without being seen and/or getting caught. As I rounded the corner, I saw a policeman pursuing Gary in the street where I had just tossed a few lit cherry bombs—it sounded as if artillery fire was exploding right in front of them! Then it was each man for himself, and we split up to make it difficult for the officers to catch us. That sounded like a good idea until I rounded the next curve and saw a patrol car coming right at me. I slowed down so as to appear that nothing was wrong, but just as I was passing by, two of the cherry bombs I had tossed exploded! Now I was on the run again, and it was like a Wild Wild West episode. I sped down alleyways, back roads, and then toward the woods, rendezvousing back at the camp. I never felt good about outrunning those officers, and I am thankful that no one was hurt along the way. God was good to get me through those times!

Why did I take you back to my good old days? To show that even a youth who seems to be far less than "righteous" may indeed be a future prophet. I share my story with you to help you remember your younger days—to remind you that you need to spend time with your kids, because if you don't, they will indeed spend time with someone else. Do not make everything seem like a sin to your children. Young people need to have fun things to do—go on outings, enjoy sporting and competition events together. Come up with some "cool" activities that include fun and travel, away from the daily routine. Youth camps are a great source of fun. I loved going to camp, and my daughters enjoyed attending summer camps for years.

No one has to grow old! We should all try to stay young and energetic and not allow our age to affect our youthfulness. My wife, Sandy, has a great perspective on thinking and acting young. She is always active, busy, and on the go—keeping God and her family foremost in her priorities.

Graduating

I loved to work, and got my first paying job when I was 12 years of age. I could be outside, meet people, and earn money to buy things that my parents could not afford or would not buy for me, depending on what I wanted. I have worked at a variety of jobs that have given me a unique education and interesting life experiences.

High school graduation was a very pivotal time for me, as it is for all young people. For me, it involved making a decision to start college, go to work, or enlist in the military. Dad insisted that if you were a male high school graduate, there were only three choices. He called it, "encouraging you to become the man God called you to be!" A lot of my friends also had these same three choices. That is why it is so hard for me to understand young people today who are still living at home with their parents when they are in their 30s and even 40s! Many of us baby boomers never had a stay-at-home fourth option, and we survived quite well.

In the months leading up to graduation, I experienced a significant renewal in my spiritual walk with the Lord. I was part of a great youth group at First Church of the Religious Charismatics.

If we could keep the old folks from running off another preacher, a preacher would stay long enough to bring in some good speakers and talk about having a "move of the Lord" in our city. During the late 1960s and early '70s, many different denominations were being filled with the Holy Spirit.

There was wonderful spiritual freedom, and all the Spirit-filled churches swelled with "Charismatic overdosed" excitement. Although our youth group members were not "hippies," we were with many who had been saved from the "true hippy movement." It was a great time to be alive—unless you were serving in Vietnam. My mandatory draft status was 1-A "wanted and holding." That meant if no college accepted me, Uncle Sam had first dibs. I was accepted at a Bible college and was ready for the Lord to enlarge my calling, since I had been "saved" about 20 more times after my blackberry wine and motorcycle days! I was excited about attending college.

Then Mom said she noticed that my heart was into expressing myself in writing. She said that during her prayer time she saw me in a university studying to write and publish God's Word. I cannot imagine many mothers encouraging their sons to drop the idea of seminary over attending a secular, state-supported college to learn a profession, especially after she heard audibly from God about my calling in life.

It is astonishing to look back at how much Mom's gentle guidance shaped my future. She did not instruct me to change my mind; she only asked that I pray about it to make sure she had heard the right message by our confirmation from the Lord. Dad was very happy because he told me all along that he knew I could preach, no doubt about it; but since he had seen a number of preachers asked to leave the church we currently attended, he said learning a trade would be a good idea. He was right again. God made it happen almost overnight; I was accepted and transferred within a week into a college that later became part of the Texas A&M university system.

College — a Time of Change

College was a brand-new experience. This was a very interesting spiritual development time for me as I began to search for my Kingdom identity, and I realized that I was becoming a stranger to the type of churches I had been raised in. Now I only enjoyed the "different" home groups and the youthful non-conventional prayer fellowships. Their focus has always stuck with me—love, acceptance, forgiveness. Because most of my classmates were not raised in seriously godly homes, they felt the "renewal" they had come to know was of serious spiritual depth. We attended large churches in Dallas on the weekends, and we would "intellectually pursue" what life in God really was all about. Bear in mind, we were a bunch of seriously hungry young people living in the "hippy movement" era.

I got along with Catholics, mostly because they were raised a lot like me—very structured. But their focus was not as fanatical as ours concerning the Holy Spirit and fire. That changed for them, like me, when they started college and the "renewal" embraced them too! I attended meetings comprised of young people from various denominations and backgrounds who were all hungry for more of the Lord. This is when I was first introduced to "real hippies"—those who were beginning to shift back into the education "establishment" without being "overly established."

Almost everyone in this group church smoked. I tried the pipe for a while, and many other things to be "cool." I never felt good about smoking, though, and knew it could harm my body—no matter what their theology taught. I don't believe smoking will cause people to lose their born-again Christian status with God but it does demonstrate a lack of self-control and willingness to be completely obedient to God and this disobedience can hinder a person's ability to hear God speak to them. Many in this group were very serious about the Lord, but some had habits that did not disappear over time. Then came "Explo '72," and the Jesus Movement! There were hippies-turned-Jesus-freaks everywhere! I was in the middle of it all, but I wasn't like them.

During that time I was searching many paths, yet I was not satisfied in any of them—until the past few years in the "prophetic movement." I was looking for my Father in a personal search that was more like a "pathetic movement." The process continued, and I met many athletes who inspired me to start lifting weights again and playing football. My younger brother had earned a full scholarship to play football for Texas Christian University, so I decided to start training and getting ready for the fall season. Unfortunately, I smashed my finger when I dropped a 300-pound barbell on it—bringing my football training efforts to a halt.

That was a tough time, almost losing my finger, but it taught me that God is a healing Father. After examination, the doctor had decided to remove the finger up to the knuckle. I was to go back for surgery in a week. In the meantime, I asked for prayer for my finger from a hometown preacher friend, Jerry Howell, who later pioneered a large church in Dallas. Immediately after Jerry prayed for my finger, I knew it was healed. When I returned to the doctor, he was surprised because the finger looked as if it was beginning to heal itself. I told him that I asked for prayer, and the doctor grinned and said, "Well, God works in mysterious ways!" Today my finger is scarred, but I have full mobility—even having the ability to type this manuscript for you and share the testimony of Jesus to the world. Again the enemy lost another battle to destroy my destiny. Everyone wants to have the use of all 10 fingers; however, pianists, surgeons, and writers especially need all their functioning fingers.

FROM HERE TO THERE

College-age kids will experiment with finding themselves. Knowing the love of the Father modeled to them by their earthly fathers will lessen the pain of the exploration. If God's agape love is not conveyed to sons and daughters, they receive a distorted view of how we are viewed by God. It seems to me that most "religious" people are worse off than most "rank and file sinners," because most are miserable people trying to live by a list of "do's and don'ts." The ones who have experienced the genuine love of an earthly father walk confidently and securely, knowing that the Lord loves them even more!

All children search for answers, and they need to know that the truth is found in the Word of God. Although my generation did not have the extreme amount of drugs and pornography available as today's kids, we had other moral temptations. As I travel and minister around the country and speak with youth, I have found that most kids want to do the right thing and not get hooked on junk. Like me in college, kids just want to be accepted by a group—but not necessarily do all the wrong things that the group may be into. I never really fit in because I chose to retain my walk with the Lord, and my determined spirit would not let the enemy into my heart to rob my future.

At the same time, I recognized a lot of hypocritical and contradictory loopholes in the lives of adult Christian leaders. Subsequently, I lost my desire to attend the "established church," especially after experiencing the excitement of young people from different countries speaking different languages who were joining together to search for the true love of the Father.

Instead of going home during summer breaks, a fellow outdoorsman and I decided to travel across the country, working on railroad contracts to pay for college. I had reached a point in my walk with the Lord when I was tired of the search for answers. I kept in touch with my family while in school and while traveling.

The more traveling I did, the more I liked it. Seeing the United States from the highway and the railway is an experience I will always treasure. Montana and Colorado are still my favorite states.

One of the most memorable experiences of the enemy almost winning by taking my life happened while I was traveling through the mountains. I was exhausted when driving my company truck back to the hotel very late one night. I awoke—divinely and abruptly—just as a solid, steel bar was about to crash through my windshield, head-on at full force. Angels must have grabbed my steering wheel, because I do not remember turning it to avoid the bar. Instantly, I heard the rearview mirror near my head snap off as the steel bar crashed through the windshield. That sound and experience was etched into my dreams for more than a few days afterward! God has spared my life many times along this journey—all in the path of processing me.

I love the mountains and the outback-rugged country fits my heart just right. However, Pennsylvania is unique, I believe, because of the godly heritage imparted by William Penn, the founder. Montana would be a dream home to my anointed "writer's den" perched off a rocky ledge; yet with family I would be most happy in the Appalachian hills of Pennsylvania. The hills of Pennsylvania offer an open Heaven for a future of hearing from God!

During my travels, I realized that I was not getting any closer to the calling I had as a child to preach and take the Word of God to the world. I hungered to hear and know more about the Lord. After college graduation, I left my "mountain man" phase behind, and returned home to Kilgore, Texas, to work as the Public Information/Public Relations director for a governmental group. This group was established as a clearinghouse for government grants that assisted many municipalities and local governments.

I returned to my church roots and attended the local Spirit-filled religious church. Many in the community from other denominations attended the different "special service" nights. During that time, I was taking a Bible course at our local community college and was introduced to a young woman who seemed to have an eye for my arrival in the same class. Not long afterward, she began attending our local church, since the pastor of the church also taught the Bible class. Before long, she was involved in all parts of my life and we became friends.

Let God Arrange Marriage

The entire church thought it was the perfect union—we were in the same place at the same time so we must be meant for each other. Surely it is God's will, they said. She was from a well-established, upper-middle-class family in our community. Her family had moved from a petroleum community in Oklahoma and rapidly built a reputation of solid, hard-working, respectable citizens who were part of a vibrant "boom town."

Although everyone was telling me that I was going to be the happiest person in the city, my heart was saying, "You don't need to do this!" There was a war going on inside my spirit; and the battle should not have included another person's life. This was when I needed a father's real love—one who prays, speaks counsel, and tells you man-to-man, "Son, if you don't love her like you have dreamed about the love of your life, then you better wait! If you have strong physical feelings but not genuine and meaningful love, and if you have *any reservations*—then put the wedding on hold! Getting married for any reason other than being God-called and ordained will not last."

This was a difficult time for me. Here I was back in my hometown and expected to assume responsibility, get married, and settle down. I did not listen to my heart and we were married. We had a rough start, and then we settled into wanting the best of all worlds.

We attended the First Religious Assembly—equivalent to a Nazareth for Jesus church. I felt as if there was a continual "tug-of-war" game for my life, and I either had to give in and get pulled across the line or let go and leave the game—my marriage. Leaving the marriage would have been a great option for all as I look back, yet the path to my current door would not have been the same, so I suppose there was a good reason for staying. But, I should have been man enough to step forward and suggest that we postpone the wedding until we received proper pastoral council. Through pastoral counseling, we would have realized the seriousness of a marriage covenant and could have discussed any reservations that we might have had. Now we were in it for "better or worse," and we learned too late the difference between a covenant (calling from God) and a vow.

Married Life

After the first year of marriage one of my dreams was born—Adam Marcus. He is the only son I have and he is a dream come true. During those few years after we were married, the Lord was dealing with me often about surrendering to the mission calling He gave me when I was 16 years of age. I was currently working as an outside salesman, traveling a large region of our state. During my sales calls I would think about what God was going to do with me now that I was married to a person who would probably never go, or stay, in the mission field. Each day the feeling to obey the call to Africa got stronger. I can still remember how unsuccessful I felt, even though I was making more money than ever before. The emptiness I felt was a result of this "mission calling" void in my life, regardless of financial gains.

I told my wife that God was calling us to go to Africa as missionaries and that we should drive to Springfield, Missouri, to talk to the staff at the missions headquarters. When we arrived in Springfield, I walked right into the department head's office and announced we were answering the call of God to go to the mission field. This isn't the usual way of beginning the process, but I decided to start at the top and work my way down. We returned home and waited for the acceptance notice. Eventually we received approval, and I was ordained in the organization as well. After holding what seemed like hundreds of services and attending every convention possible, we raised enough monthly support for us to go to Africa.

Telling my wife's folks where we were going was like telling them we were headed to the moon! Her family was very caring, and here I was about to take away their only daughter and their new grandson to live in Africa. Everything happened very quickly and off we flew to Malawi, a small country in East Africa.

From the very first day on the mission field, life was totally different from anything we had ever known before. After we received a briefing to acclimate us to the culture, a man working in the yard next door was bitten by a black mamba snake. I was the one who took this poor soul to the hospital, although I had no clue where I was, what language they spoke, or how to drive on the opposite side of the road. Only God knows how we made it to Queen Anne's Hospital in Blantyre! I prayed and believed that the man would not die. The doctor gave him a shot and said it was really only an "experiment" to see if he would survive or not. The next day this man was back raking leaves—barefoot—in the same location where he had been bitten the day before. "Welcome to Africa!" they said to me.

Our house was not quite ready to live in, so I helped do much of the inside finish work. I attended language school in Dedza to learn the language of the people I would be ministering to. Dedza is located in the tea-growing region of the country. While I was attending language school, our second child was born—a beautiful little girl we named Amy Marie. Now we had a boy and a girl and were part of a small group of missionaries serving in a very small country that was oceans away from family and friends.

Near where we lived there was a road that served as a boundary between Malawi and Mozambique. At that time Mozambique was controlled by a Marxist regime known for its brutality. Because I was unable to enter Mozambique, I decided to run along that road every morning at 6 A.M. and in Jesus' name decree them a Christian nation. Many prayed for that country over the years, and thankfully in the early 1990s the first free elections were held after years of violence and political turmoil.

Life was very different from the way we lived in the United States. For example, I came down with malaria and almost died during treatment—and we only had electricity a few hours each night that was generator-produced. This was a tough assignment in many ways.

Once I was asked to go to South Africa with another missionary to purchase a pickup truck to be used in our ministry work.

Before beginning our long drive back to Malawi, we loaded it with supplies. As we approached the Limpopo River Bridge that separates Zimbabwe from Zambia, we were stopped by heavily armed men who jumped in front of our truck and demanded we back up and read the sign posted. We could not read the sign because it was written in a foreign-to-us language, but we found out that we were supposed to stop and wait until our vehicle was inspected before proceeding toward the bridge.

We were about 500 miles away from "civilization," and I knew we could be in serious trouble if we said or did anything to upset these men. Under my breath I was praying in the Spirit. The men walked around the truck but did not untie the tarp. When the lead soldier came to my window and asked for cigarettes, it was a miracle that we had a case of chocolate bars on the floor of the truck. When I gave it to him, he dropped his machine gun that was aimed directly at my head, and I was praying it would not go off as it hit the ground!

The gun-wielding soldier was probably around 15 years old, dressed in camouflage fatigues, and seemed to be the guy in charge. With chocolates in hand, he grinned from ear to ear and motioned us to drive over the river bridge.

That was just one of many miracles that happened while I was in Africa—I have a very fond heart for that land. Many people came to accept the Lord as their Savior through the press we had there, and multiplied thousands of tracts were distributed across the region.

Going Home

But the enemy bombarded us from all sides with different and constant attacks. The people who were supposed to be working *with* us actually planned our entire future—and the plans they made did not line up with what God was telling us to do. But mostly the evil one worked through the weak relationship between me and my wife. She was extremely homesick for her mother and father. Finally she said she was going home with or without me. Of course I wanted to be with my wife and children, so we left the mission field halfway through our commitment.

Less than two years in the mission field, and we were headed back home. We cited every excuse in the book—many very real and typical of mission field norms. Upon arrival back in the United States, I felt a tinge of hope that our marriage was going to be OK. However, living with her folks for a season because our house was not available right away caused even more troubles. We joined the Presbyterian Church that her parents were members of, and as it was, new faces and new opportunities arose. I took off and up in business as a representative in the banking equipment profession and traveled across a large portion of the state.

During that time of transition into the business world from returned missionary hero gone AWOL, I felt my life was losing purpose. My spirit was silently screaming, "Get me out of here!" Yet I was a failed minister. Church members who knew me were kind to my face, but I felt we were the "scuttlebutt" floating around inside the community religious circles. This was a very difficult time for me.

Suddenly I was facing a tidal wave with such a strong undercurrent that it almost took me out to sea with no hope of return. Trying to be a good husband became the biggest battle of my life. The harder I tried, the more I felt like a failure. I was so young, and our hometown so small that the entire community had time to daily review my defeats.

One day right before I was leaving to attend a week-long business meeting in another city, my wife told me she wanted a divorce. I was shocked. I will never forget it—I felt as if my life was being destroyed. When I returned from the trip, we separated. I just took off and snapped—it was too much to handle. I was losing my dreams, years of hopes and plans. People looked to me to produce a return on their investment in me, and they had reaped nothing but failure. I was haunted night and day by my lack of achievement and failures—my marriage and my calling to the mission field.

I moved into an apartment that was about 30 minutes west of our town to try to sort things out on my own. Instead of turning to my heavenly Father, who would never consider me a loser, I tried to create a reality I could live with. I started hanging out with the business crowd at happy hour, and found a sense of belonging in this new social climate. I was playing hide and seek in the corporate world system, learning how to maneuver people. I knew that my career would be enhanced if I joined the social hour meetings with the officers and the vice presidents of the organizations I was wooing. It was comforting for a season to shift the pressure of an unhappy marriage and unfulfilled expectations to a successful career environment. It wasn't total peace, yet it beat what had been around the previous corner.

HONESTY

My private life was so out of control that I could have well been the Samarian *man* at the well that day Jesus asked for a drink. I never planned to be the example to show others how *not* to do life, but I have to be honest. Although my human nature wants me to "gloss over" those problem times, my heart pushes me to bare it all so you can read it and weep. I hope that you will not only cry with me, but that you will learn from my mistakes. "Don't do as I did, do as I say!" I feel much consolation knowing that everyone who reads this "tell all" story of

mine will take advantage of my dying to self and becoming resurrected to a new life.

Thank God for transformation! Yes, I was a selfish, lying
make-believe who was headed straight to a sinner's hell for
being filled with so much knowledge, yet not having enough
common sense to repent or backbone to withstand the battles of
the evil one during the raging war. What happened when the
barrage of the enemy's forces came after my strong mantle that
was truly placed there by God before I was even born? I ran
from the fight. By doing so, I lost my identity and hid from the
life that God gave me. I allowed the enemy, at least temporarily,
to kill, steal, and destroy my destiny.

Have you ever experienced a time when your pet has been
hurt and it bites or scratches you when you try to help it? That
is how I viewed people's offer of help during that time in my
life. Defeat loomed in every corridor. I allowed reason to go out
to sea and went along, hoping to find something better to cling
to. During that process, as the divorce was being filed and papers served, all I saw was destruction and pain. Not wanting to
consider any of it in depth, I just signed whatever was handed
to me and moved on about my new life. That is until one day
when I received a call saying that if I did not pay an exorbitant
amount of back child support payments—I would be thrown in
jail. What?! I was shocked—again. I was already regularly paying the interim amount we had agreed upon, and there was not
much left over for my own living expenses.

Thinking back, I had as much love for my first wife as my
heart could provide under the circumstances. Only much later
and much further down the trail of trials would I eventually
discover my God-awarded "true love." None except the Father
can show you His destiny for you. If you believe that, and allow

the Father to adjust your heart to receive His complete love, then you will discover it.

God's unconditional love has "no strings attached." That is what causes us to fear it; yet, that is what we are all desperate to find. Think *relationship*. This kind of love must be first based upon your *relationship* with the eternal Father. Most of us do not understand the security of a real loving relationship displayed by a loving earthly father. All my life, it seemed I was a lost boy looking for that love. The genuine love of the real Father. Unconditional love with no strings attached.

LIFE ON THE OUTSIDE

Mostly because my nerves, emotions, and life were in an uncontrollable tailspin, I took off for the hills and the trees. I had to get away to a place where I did not have to deal with lawyers, courts, and threats, and could focus on the land and nature. I moved into a hidden cabin to think about what I was going to do next. During this time I became very involved with business people who used my marketing skills to their advantage. The crowd I was a part of would do whatever it took to take care of one of its own—and no one could serve me a warrant where I lived now. I was in a self-protection frame of mind.

Somehow, though, my now ex-wife figured out how to have my mother get a message to me. The message: if I would turn myself in, I could get the child support worked out before the Christmas holidays. I had a very uneasy feeling about this deal, but thought that I was now too well connected to be cornered and/or jailed. I did the right thing, and in a new company vehicle, drove to my ex-wife's office to handle the details of rectifying the child support issue.

When I arrived at her office, I was told that she was out. While I waited, I was asked to write a list of things to get the kids for Christmas and to work out the details of how I was planning to pay the overdue child support payments. My gut feelings and early-childhood prophetic mantle of God told me something was wrong. As I turned to leave, the deputy sheriff was waiting at the door, and I was arrested and taken to the county jail. I was permitted to remove my personal belongings from the company truck, and I realized then that not only would I lose my new job and my only means of transportation, but now I had no way to pay the child support that I owed.

I was at the end of my senses, and for the first few days in jail, I remember staring at the people who were wondering what I was doing there. My stare made it clear that I was not one to tangle with! I can't even imagine what I would have done if I was pushed just one more inch. That was a tough time in my life! I was at the bottom. Sitting in that little cell, I kept wondering what was going to happen to me. That is when I decided to never go back to "church" again. If I could end up in jail after serving on a mission field all because I couldn't afford to pay some back child support, then I did not want anything to do with religion.

Eventually I was assigned to a work release program, and I went directly back to the hidden cabin in the woods and to the same crowd—the crowd who knew more about family and taking care of their own than any church member I had known up to that point. Church wasn't much more than a religious game in my mind.

Most of the time we were living on the edge—we all carried handguns for "life insurance." This was life in rural Texas. It's the same today, but not as visible. We had business in Louisiana and hung with people who had connections with the former Louisiana governor, and others I cannot mention. At times I felt like a Clyde Barrow of Bonnie and Clyde fame, especially driving the '47 model tricked out Chevy we had.

I learned a lot about basic survival on the streets. We got into gambling and burglary to get cash to pay the bills. I was helping some pretty rough people during that time, and then I got word that the county legal officers listened to my mom's sister who came in from Las Vegas to help untangle the child support mess. I had three choices: 1. give all my life's savings and a lump sum per month to my ex-wife; 2. go back to jail; or, 3. sign sole custody of our children over to her. That was not going to work.

I walked outside and had counsel from my stepfather and my aunt from Vegas. They both advised me to sign, as "ink will never outweigh blood." They advised that it could only get worse the longer the situation went unresolved. This was a very painful decision, but I gave up Adam Marcus, my only son, and Amy, my daughter. My ex-wife married an engineer, and the children's names were changed to reflect her new family.

All in all, even though this experience hurt terribly, I knew it was best for all of us; because I did not know what I was looking for yet or what I might do from day to day. I was looking for answers and trying to make sense out of the trail my life was on.

One time I was working on a bank deal with some friends and an associate drove up in his Mercedes Benz. He popped open the trunk lid, and inside was enough cocaine to sink a fishing boat! I knew this amount was way beyond recreational—it was occupational. Wow! My mind was racing but I wasn't showing it. Just being there could get me killed and/or implicated for something I did not have anything to do with.

My life had drastically changed from only a few years earlier when I was sharing the love of Jesus in Africa.

Buying and Selling

I started working with "Boss Hog" in a little town and I began earning more "respectable" money. Real estate was a booming business, and we took advantage of it. We had it all—houses, farms, thousands of acres to roam, lots of wine, women, and song. All I wanted was to absorb myself in the respectable business of dirt and trees. I believe God gave me a knack for selling land, and we bought and sold most of North and East Texas a time or two. Friends in the mountains told me their "white lightning" business operated much like our group did.

I had no wife, no children, and I had no child support to pay, but I did have a handful of pictures of my past life, and lots of Jim Beam whiskey. I poured myself into the land deals and because we owned a few banks, the deals got easier. It was especially nice having our own title company. To make matters even better, Boss Hog was a three-time state legislator from the district, so this was a good area for us to live and do business. We had parties and took trips to Vegas. I was making more money than I ever imagined. We played poker on many a cold winter night with the local boys and, of course, the local police chief. He would laugh about hiding the stack of paperwork he had on me.

The more you go with the ways of the world, the more the world gets you hooked into its system. I remember preachers saying that the heavily traveled road is tempting and wide. Before the boss knew it—we were in a jam—situations can change very quickly in the world. The "feds" stepped into the picture and then it all got messy. People were busted for delivering and/or selling large amounts of dope—some of them had connections to Boss Hog's bank or his other interests. We were not involved in drugs, but some of our associates were making it tough for us to keep out of the federal fray.

Again, at the expense of sparing some names and details, I can assure you that God used this time to underscore to me the frailty of life. I remember more than once when the barrels of loaded guns, the size of four-inch pipes, looked me in the eyes. God had to have saved me! God is merciful, yet God needs us to be processed and thankful for His mercy. When I deserved no way out, God sent many messengers at the continual requests of praying parents and loved ones to remove the grip of back alley deals from my life. When I survey the wonders of His grace, I often question how much misery we choose to add to our pathways. All I can say is that some of my near-eternity trips were probably not God's ideas for processing. If we are given the grace to get out of these situations, the memory adds a bonus to the blender.

The land business was a steady market, no matter what else came and went. I was feeling more secure during this time and thought about settling down. One day I walked into Boss Hog's bank—he was always in the middle of a closing or something. As I waited for him, I noticed an attractive teller. I pointed out the woman to Boss Hog and he said she was married. Disappointed, I forgot about her and kept busy making more land deals.

A few months later, one of our office staff told me that a young woman was going through a bad divorce and needed a friend. She asked if I would be interested in accompanying her to the local festival. I said sure. The young woman in need of a friend turned out to be the same woman I was attracted to at Boss Hog's bank. When we walked through the park, I felt as if she was the one I wanted to marry. After only a few weeks I asked her to marry me. She did not give me an answer right away; but in a few days she called me and accepted my proposal. Without inquiring of God, we got married entirely too quickly by a very new and nervous Justice of the Peace; I would have been nervous too if I knew then what would happen later!

It was a wild time for me to be getting married again. I was not a good candidate for the job of husband, but she was unaware of my past. She was a nice woman, tenderhearted compared to my first wife, and she was a member of the Baptist church. I got off to a rocky start with her two children; and her ex-husband was a little too fresh of an "ex" to think that it was a good idea for her to get married again so soon. He had not given up on the idea that they would get back together. We had a few fisticuffs in the yard, and we both realized that our relationship was not going to be amicable.

Life to me was what I made of it. I believed that being "the nice person" had cost me my dreams, wife and kids, ministry, friends, church, and hometown. Now I wanted to be the smartest and strongest person. Nobody in my old world understood my new life, because they had learned how to settle or play the game—or enjoyed living in their rut (rut: a long grave with both ends kicked out!).

I decided we should move with the company closer to the larger cities and to my hometown. The real estate market took a terrible dive during that time, due to rising interest rates and inflation. It was time for a change, and I moved out of the business connection circle that had become my family for a season. Not long afterward they contacted me and said that Boss Hog had committed suicide in a local hotel room. I was puzzled about his cause of death. He was a close friend, and I have never been fully convinced that it was suicide. The others said to let it go and many, including the FBI, assured us that he indeed took his own life. Nonetheless, it has never been settled in my heart of hearts.

Settled in a new area, my wife and I started life together. Unfortunately, it included my selfishness and my frequent hunting time in the woods. The stepchildren, especially the son, purposely tried to make things difficult. I got increasingly more miserable at the way life was going. Nothing I did in business or otherwise satisfied me. I was very lonely and felt sorry for involving my second wife in my life of rejection and hurt. Bitterness develops when you are always mad and grinding an axe about not doing the right thing or not dealing with a rejection early on. When that happens, all you want to do is to make everyone around you bitter and angry—just like you are.

The best thing about my second marriage is that we had two beautiful girls, Raegan and Allison. Both were born into a life where Dad wanted to be free and Mom wanted to be loved. Unfortunately for her and for the children, she married me on the rebound, and even in the best settings, it is difficult to make a marriage work based on a desperate attempt to make up for a past mistake. It was mostly my fault though; not having a relationship with the love of the Father displayed in my life gave me more reason to latch onto anything I could find for help. I did not know where to find help for my broken spirit. The church offered prayer; others gave advice about how to be happy and full of joy like them—it always seemed like a game to me.

My second wife's time was now totally absorbed in raising babies, and she had two older children at home as well. I threw myself into my new job selling frozen food all across East Texas. It was during this time when we started living a little better as a family and attended church more often. I would go through phases of wanting to live for the Lord, and then the attacks began.

Every time we would get into church, the devil would pull me right back into the lifestyle of weekend play with the guys. I was not willing to make the changes I heard about in church that I should "die" and live for Jesus.

If you are playing hide and seek with God—like I was—know that He loves you no matter what! The church may or may not have the right answers for you, but let me assure you that God's Word never lies and His love never dies! You will die, however, in this process of becoming. When you assume you carry as much power as God and play religious compromise games—you will have to die to self to become the person He wants you to be.

Yes—dying can be a good thing!

CHAPTER 3

A Time To Die

There is a time for everything, and a season for every activity under Heaven: A time to be born and a time to die, a time to plant and a time to uproot (Ecclesiastes 3:1-2 NIV).

God has set times for all seasons of our destiny. Whether or not we move willingly in them affects the proper outcome. Nonetheless, just as we have been born, so shall we one day leave this world and partake of eternal life. Where you spend eternity depends on the choices you make on this earth. Choose life more abundantly. Say "yes" to the Father!

Now that I was living near home once again and enjoying some resemblance of a normal lifestyle, God began dealing with me about the past. Because I had not dealt with the rejection and the bitterness, it would not disappear—out of sight is not out of your mind. Our human psyche will go along with our mental attempts to deny existence, yet during life's calamities, the hard drive of our spirit-person will go into deep reference to find many hidden secrets. Denial only leads to build up, and the continued grinding on your mind and body will take a physical as well as spiritual toll.

As career doors opened, an opportunity to join a new medical services company appeared. It was an excellent opportunity to progress within the area of my expertise. I believe that God opened this door, and through it many new associations began to develop in my spiritual and corporate networking environment. My self-esteem slowly returned, and we returned to regular church attendance. Although I knew in my heart that we were not "home" yet, I was getting a lot closer on this road than on the detour I had taken years ago.

We were experiencing what I considered God's gradual path of restoration in our lives. This was a good time for us. We lived in a nice city, our kids were attending a great school system, and our lifestyle was easy and relaxed—no looking over my shoulder or remembering past failures. Life was a lot better!

Dying Was Not on My Schedule

Having survived all the self-inflicted and demon-inflicted destruction, I was now looking at life with hope. I hoped that God would offer me another opportunity to become "complete." God's view of your life and your view of your life are two completely different perspectives. Our religious mind-set tells us there will be a gradual winding pathway up the spiraling ascension to God's betterment for our destiny. Not so. The way we think can never predicate the way the Father views us. The arm of flesh does not appropriate the will of God.

People will offer many solutions to problems based simply on a good approach to make a bad situation better. That is not altogether incorrect thinking. However, God will manifest Himself in the natural through us to the degree we submit to Him and His plan. God never authorized my carnal attempts to accomplish His plans.

By now the company was booming, and God was giving me great favor and increase for the corporation. Although we seemed to be experiencing steady financial growth, the closer the Lord would draw me in, the more the warfare at the corporate level increased. No amount of success would appease the "subsurface spiritual rivalry" that intensified with every business and financial boost.

One day while visiting my mother in her weakening health condition, I asked her what was happening with her spiritually, because she always had great spiritual discernment. Upon hearing my case of the associated spiritual warfare in spite of the financial success, she said it was most likely a demonic base in the company that was jealous of the destiny God was about to bring into my life. She explained that it was based in a spirit realm aligned with the occult, and therefore no matter how great my performance, the darkness would never allow me to be rewarded unless I bowed to it. This was difficult to hear because I knew that God had placed me there, and the proof had been displayed in my life through increased hunger to move closer to the Father. When spiritual inventory grows, it has always been my experience that God's favor of financial provision is a great indicator of His blessings and approval.

However, there was a constant dark spiritual undertow no matter how much I prayed, drew nearer to God, faithfully tithed, or gave to the Kingdom of God. It became apparent that God brought us favor everywhere He placed my feet. The warfare increased to the point that while at the health club one day I asked a friend and trainer who was a former Navy Seal about it. I asked him what he saw in combat against the "jealous spirit" applied to the hand that fed it. He said it was his experience that these spirits always want more and will never allow us to become the disciplined person required to accomplish the goal.

This was not a "churchy" answer but one from a man who was a pure disciple and leader of human discipline. Navy Seals are that and more! This guy's middle name is "Discipline" with a capital D! He could smell excuses before they were spoken! Yes, his answer was correct—the natural and the spiritual answers agreed. The spiritual warfare involved an individual, undisciplined person who felt threatened because what God was offering him was not enjoyed from his spiritual base. Eventually the pressure became insurmountable, and it then became obvious that the owner's wife was the one pushing the buttons.

When dealing with the demonic realm, you cannot reason from the godly point of view. After all was eventually revealed, someone gave me a prophetic word of warning that God was going to take me through a very necessary spiritual growth step that would cause me to "die" to all my ways and myself. I was supposed to embrace the new shift into God's fivefold ministry calling that had become dormant within me. That prophetic word hit the bull's eye of my target! However, dying was not on my calendar—but it was on God's!

O death, where is thy sting? O grave, where is thy victory?
(1 Corinthians 15:55 KJV).

It was like any day in my office. Schedules and calendars of events in the medical profession direct the lifestyle. It is the "nature of the beast" to live by appointment calendars in the corporate world, yet even more so in the medical climate.

This day included presenting a huge display that I had arranged for our company to be directly in the middle of for exposure in that market. As was the norm, the owner's wife wanted to be involved in anything that focused immediate attention and act as if she was instrumental in pulling it all together. That did not bother me, though, because the owner always has the right to decide when and where to appear on behalf of the company. The problem arose this day because she purposefully chose to criticize and destroy the work that had been designed to bring future business success. It was paramount that everything go along smoothly this day. Remember the spiritual backdrop. Well, all that *could* go wrong *did*, and no matter the amount of planning, I could not win on that playing field.

As the events unfolded, I hurried to the newspaper office to place an ad before the deadline. While I was driving, I had a very strong feeling of heaviness sink into my gut. I could not shake it off. Upon visiting briefly with my regular customer service person, the entire bottom seemed to fall out from under me. I looked up and the room began to spin. I had just eaten a quick lunch on the run and it was very fresh, so I knew my lightheadedness was not food related.

I remembered having a similar feeling when I had arrived to finalize the details with the owner's wife at the display earlier. With a contorted facial countenance, she made it clear that no matter how successful I thought the display would be, she would ensure its destruction. This was the jealousy that my mother had identified and my Navy Seal friend had defined.

No Weapon Formed Against You Will Prosper

"Ma'am I feel sick," I told the advertising customer service representative.

"I gave you the best price as usual!" she said.

"Ma'am, my head is spinning and the room is going in circles."

She looked at me and blurted out, "You look sick!"

"Yes ma'am, that's what I'm trying to tell you."

"Lay your head on my desk while I go get some help," she commanded.

I remember feeling weird about laying my head on her desk, thinking it would soon pass and that this was too much attention for a bout of passing nausea. However, I only remember what happened next in bits and pieces.

I woke up briefly and saw lots of commotion going on in the newspaper office, while simultaneously I felt a lifting sensation. The EMS technicians were lifting me upward onto a stretcher. It was time for my first ambulance ride. One of my younger twin sisters was a registered nurse for our company, and she arrived and rode with me in the ambulance. She was trying to talk to me, asking me to chew on a candy bar. I remember how trying to chew made breathing so much more difficult. Breathing! Wow! I felt as if I was not getting any air.

The next thing I remember is waking up with a huge light shining directly down on my face. I must be in the emergency room—then everything seemed to be happening in slow motion. Drifting in and out of consciousness, I looked around at one point and recognized all my loved ones and family gathered around me. I wondered if I was at a family reunion.

As I looked up, I heard my dad saying, "Son, you are not going home before me! Now wake up and come to life!" This did not seem normal for him to be telling me I was not supposed to die! Was that it? Was I dying?

The next time I woke, I saw a very concerned look on a doctor's face that made me wonder what was happening in this room full of frantically busy specialists. I heard my sister, the nurse, explain to Mother that from tests they ran on me, I had less than 45 percent of the regular oxygen count in my blood. Although I was breathing, no oxygen was getting to the necessary location—me! That is about as basic as it gets.

Once again coming slowly around, seemingly almost gone, I felt my rough-cut maintenance mechanic father holding my hand and heard him talking to me. When I opened my eyes, I thought I was dreaming because Dad had never held my hand. He had lived a very hard life and that was just the way he was raised—no touching. Now I realized in my spirit that this was not a good scene. Dad seemed desperate when he said, "You are not going to leave us, son!" I felt very sickened in my body, too weak to move, and gasping to hang on for another second. I looked into my father's eyes and said, "Good-bye Dad, I am leaving you now."

Then I passed on from life to death immediately. I was in a tunnel and saw the light getting dim and farther away. Yes, that is exactly what I saw. When the light disappeared from my tunnel, I had a "blinking" light switch coming on feeling, and then it became, for a split second, a solid "white screen" on my life's video viewer.

DEAD TO THIS WORLD!

Dying is something you cannot schedule; yet, death will rearrange all your schedules.

After the white screen flashed by, I looked up and saw everyone and everything in the emergency room. I felt better at that moment than ever before. Because I had no more pain in my physical body, I felt perfect.

I asked what all the alarm was about. But nobody answered me. Again I asked my family why they were worried about that body on the table when I was perfectly well and sitting up next to it. I could not get a response; and then I felt my spirit begin to rise above them in the same room. I hovered there for a little while and again asked them the question to see if they would respond.

I said good-bye faintly and then felt as if I was being raised upward and onward. The movement upward would be comparable to taking an open cockpit helicopter ride above the immediate area. This part was fun. Once I kept moving upward, I felt very peaceful; then darkness started approaching. This disturbed me and immediately I wanted to escape, but I kept moving toward the middle of the darkness as I was in a continual ascent.

I looked up and from nowhere appeared large ghoulish beings of monstrous proportion that were at war with huge men with bronze-colored skin and swords drawn, fighting fiercely. The men were winning but the battle was not an easy one! I knew immediately that they were God's warring angels, and this must be the warfare in the heavenlies just above the earthly realm.

> *Then said he unto me, Fear not, Daniel: for from the first day that thou didst set thine heart to understand, and to chasten thyself before thy God, thy words were heard, and I am come for thy words* (Daniel 10:12 KJV).

When the warfare became intense, I crouched into a fetal position to create some kind of defense for myself. I wondered if this was to be my hell because of the way I had lived much of my life.

Seeing Heaven

What I am about to recount is my own personal experience. It may be different from the way you view Heaven from the Bible's perspective. I have shared my testimony a few times with church and other group audiences, and a few people have told me that I was in "paradise," not Heaven. However, I know where God took me, and it was indeed Heaven.

Finally looking up from my curled position, I saw that I had continued moving up above the warfare realm. What a relief. On occasion, even now, I pray and thank God for His agents who are strategically placed on vigilant assignment over His Kingdom and citizenship. We are so blessed that God has every detail worked out for our benefit. After being in Heaven, I pray the Lord's Prayer from a different perspective—especially, *"Thy Kingdom come, Thy will be done* **on earth as it is in Heaven.**"

I saw gorgeous mountains appear everywhere, and suddenly I realized that God had every detail planned for my homecoming. The Father knew that I loved the mountains and dreamed of living in a lodge in the middle of a mountain one day. This sight was a snow-capped blessing that only a caring and loving Father would give His child.

As my view of the snow-covered peaks became more brilliant and I got closer and closer, it was obvious that I was either going to crash into one or would just barely clear the top. I came right up to the top of those splendid heaps of snowy crests and then swerved right between two peaks and flew through to the other side of the range. Oh, what a beautiful sight.

Heaven has never been my ministry theme on this earth; however, I have a much greater appreciation for it now. These views were like none I had ever witnessed. Seeing the Lord's magnificent creation was an experience worth dying for! Not like Fudge Nut Chocolate Ice Cream Brownie Delight is "to die for." No—this was *much* better. Heaven's scenery is breathtakingly beautiful—too beautiful to describe in anything less than an entire book.

The view as I was ascending the mountain range can best be described in earthly terms as the brilliance of millions of dazzling lights in multishades of radiance. As topping on the snow-topped mountain cake of luminosity, thousands and thousands of colorful onion-dome rooftops were scattered along each ridge. Similar to the ones seen on Russian churches, these were exotically golden to the degree beyond 24-karat sparkling sheen, and they radiated from the reflection of the other brilliant lights shining from every angle. In each of the rooftops were slim slits of vertical windows reaching nearly to the top of each with at least four per rooftop.

Instead of moving upward as had been the case since leaving the emergency room, I froze as I suddenly realized that I was moving slowly downward just after I passed what seemed to be a very large city. I landed gently on my feet in front of a huge gate. Staring at the gate's beauty and feeling an indescribable comfort, I naturally reached out and touched the panel on the gate. It looked and felt like the most spectacular solid layer of mother-of-pearl I had ever seen. The entire pearl panel was a pure creamy white with just enough swirls in it to give it a rich texture. As my hand moved across the surface, I realized that the 40- to 50-foot tall gate was majestically made of *one solid piece* of perfectly formed mother-of-pearl. As you no doubt know, mother-of-pearl is the internal layer of certain (usually small) mollusk shells—only God could create such a gate.

Only then did my spirit recognize that I was in Heaven. I remembered reading about the pearly gates and golden cities in the

Bible. This is Heaven! No wonder I did not have adequate words to describe the dazzling beauty surrounding me. My pathetic descriptions pale compared to what I saw and what you too will one day experience. I looked down and saw I was standing on a street made of pure gold. The gold was approximately 18-24 inches thick and it was so pure it was like looking into golden honey that is almost transparent. Standing inside the gate was not the same as on the other side of the gate—I was inside, in Heaven. My presence of mind was becoming clearer and I knew that my experience was not a vision—it wasn't about being "caught up" in a dream about Heaven. It was real. God was allowing me to see Heaven in all its brilliance and intensity.

When you consider earth's beauty, it is just that. When you view for the first time Heaven's brilliance, you will understand what I am saying about the difference. *Vividness* describes the color wheel in Heaven. There are thousands of colors in Heaven that we have never seen before, probably because vision is enhanced tremendously as our spiritual eyes are opened. Our finite minds cannot even *imagine* the beauty of God's sparkling scenery. This is a trip worth making—don't miss Heaven!

Now I felt the warmth of my Lord Jesus drawing my spirit to Himself. Though this experience could fill volumes, I will share only a portion now. The drawing of His heart to mine created a feeling of love and bliss that almost defies description. I know it involved my submitting and subsequently being drawn to His Glorious Being. It wasn't the way I had imagined while on earth, as I had expected to throw myself at Him. Instead, a gentle, joyful, blissful peace came so calmly and easily. I felt an air of humble respect that just the memory of it evokes precious emotions. There was an immeasurable tenderness in Jesus' Spirit. I gained new insights about being "drawn unto the Lord." He wants us to feel deep in our spirits, and I can testify that my senses were very keen while in Heaven.

As I stood motionless in the presence of Jesus; I felt the presence of another being near me. It felt heavenly; almost like now when my wife, Sandy, quietly walks in the room while I am making coffee and I can feel her there but did not hear her come in. I turned to see who the other person was, hoping to catch a glimpse of Elijah or Samuel or Moses. But instead it was a young man with a face that looked very much like mine. "You must be Stanley!" I recognized him and knew in my spirit before ever saying a word that it was my brother—the brother I had never known.

Stanley smiled at me, "Yes, Mark, I am Stanley. Welcome to Heaven!"

Then I remembered a conversation I had with my mother when I was very young. I found a toy that I had never seen before. Mother told me to put it back where I found it because it had belonged to my older brother.

"Where is my brother?" I asked.

"He's in Heaven with Jesus," she said. She told me that when my brother was very young, he was hit by a car when he was crossing the road to play with some friends at the creek near our home. He died soon after the accident; I believe she said that he died in her arms. She cried, and I hugged her. We never mentioned Stanley again, and I never even saw a picture of him.

Heavenly Reunions

"Are we really here, brother, in Heaven, and this is not a dream or vision?" I asked my big brother.

"No, you are not in a third heaven, you are in Heaven!" he said.

As we stood there together, I had so many questions to ask him, but he answered them before I even asked! He knew what I wanted to ask him. That was too cool! In the middle of another thought, he finished my sentence… "I know, you want to go sit at Jesus' feet and thank Him for showing you love and mercy, right?"

"Yes, brother, you got it right again!"

Even though I could actually feel the peace of His presence surrounding everything and permeating my spirit, I felt I had to be closer to my Savior. I *did* want to go see Jesus and was actually feeling drawn to Him the entire time Stanley and I were talking. I had a deep yearning to thank Him constantly, because He forgave me and saved me and gave me Heaven—because I knew I deserved hell. Yes, when I accepted Jesus, the fear of hell was over. When we repent and serve the Savior, we have hope—oh, what a joy divine!

Now Stanley asked the questions. I could not read all his thoughts, but I knew most of them before he asked. "Did you know that God wants you to be obedient to His calling and will for your life?"

"Yes," I replied.

"Did God not name you by His audible voice while in *our* mother's womb?"

"Oh, wow, there are certainly no secrets up here! Absolutely He did, Stanley."

Then Stanley said, "God sent me here to talk to you and give you some instructions, because you are one who needs it said unmistakably clearly, and now you will be without any excuse!"

A LITTLE TALK WITH JESUS

I was listening intently to Stanley because his last statement got my attention. I did not know what he meant, but I knew it was important; so I waited anxiously for what he had to say next.

"God called you by name and spoke aloud to *our* mother; and He later told you that you would be a voice to the nations and would one day obey—did those things not happen?"

If you think for a moment that I had any defenses or replies, forget it! I was without an excuse up there. I was naked and transparent to the last corpuscle of my soul. As I stood there before Stanley, it was obvious that we were going to have a little further discussion!

He continued, "You are not here for the whole tour or to stay. You are here to get a direct message from the Father through me as an indisputable messenger and witness that you will, for sure, be able to recall and know that you must obey His voice."

I listened very carefully. "Mark, my brother, the Lord created and called you, and you will now be completely without excuse as you return to earth. God says He wants you to always remember two things as you go to the nations as His voice: 1. You must let them know that we are all called to share the name of Jesus with the world. God says that when you take His name as your Savior; you have taken upon yourself the assignment to share what you received with all you meet." Matthew 10:8 came to my mind as Stanley was speaking, *"freely ye have received, freely give."*

Stanley continued, telling me that God said, "The second is equal to the first in requirements. 2. Incorporate the power of agreement in prayer with my people. You cannot truly come into the *power of agreement* until you bring into focus the prayer Jesus prayed and which was recorded in the Bible."

Unity is the way the power of agreement works. Incorporate the power of unity and thus you will be able to tap into the forsaken benefits that have *never been accessed*.

The Power of Unity

Wow! What Stanley told me almost knocked me over. Yes, Jesus actually did pray that prayer:

> *My prayer is not for them alone. I pray also for those who will believe in me through their message, that* **all of them may be one, Father, just as you are in me and I am in you.** *May they also be in us so that the world may believe that you have sent me. I have given them the glory that you gave me, that they may be one as we are one* (John 17:20-22 NIV, emphasis added).

Many of us have never accessed the depth of power that comes from the glory of Jesus living in total unity with the Father, nor have we demonstrated this glorious power through signs, wonders and miracles. Yet the greatest of all gifts is the true love that cannot be understood outside the unity that He is describing.

Stanley looked at me, and said, "John Mark, you will complete this mission, and you will make *our mother* proud. You will also please our Father God. You will not be alone. God is giving you all you need and will speak to you often."

A wave of blessed assurance overwhelmed me, as I had never before experienced. Then I realized my brother was telling me that I was going back. "Stanley, wait, I want to ask you a couple of questions. Am I seeing all of Heaven right now?"

"No, Mark," Stanley replied. He pointed to a tiny spot on his fingernail and said, "You do not yet have a true concept of *huge*! As far as the eye can see, in every direction is more of Heaven. You are only seeing a small portion. There are many more gates leading to other enormous areas of Heaven. One day you will see all of it, but now you must return to earth to complete your assignment."

"No, wait a minute, please Stanley. I want to ask you another question."

He smiled, as if knowing me so well. "OK, John Mark, what is it you want to know?"

"All those cities I saw on my way in here, they were so brilliant and seemed like a never-ending ocean horizon, what are the names of those cities?"

He started laughing and said, "Brother, those are not *cities*, those are *mansions*!" "Mansions?"

Glory Mansions

In my Father's house are many mansions: if it were not so, I would have told you. I go to prepare a place for you" (John 14:2 KJV).

Here I was—in Heaven—discussing the mansions that Jesus talked about. Here they were right in front of me! My mind was in overload.

"John Mark Pool, my dear brother, you must return now. God has given you an important message: to be His voice to the nations and to encourage people to share the name of Jesus with others. God knows you will take the message of the Father's heart to be one with Him as He is one with the Son, Jesus Christ. Incorporate the power of agreement of prayer because, remember, it breaks the stronghold of the enemy. If we do not use this power, the enemy will use it against us!"

Like Mary, the mother of Jesus, I pondered in my heart all that he told me.

"No excuses now," I smiled and said to Stanley.

"John Mark, you really have to get back because our family is praying in the power of agreement over your healing right now; but as you go, there is one more thing you must know. The enemy had an assignment to kill you, and God allowed it to bring you before the throne. Now you must be especially careful to obey. Do not be afraid of the power of the enemy, as the Father gives him the only power he has and that will soon be removed! God is all powerful—tell this to the people of the nations, and the world will be changed for His glory."

Knowing that it was time to return, I leaned over and we hugged tightly. Stanley softly said, "John Mark, one of those huge mansions has your name at the top of it! Go now with God; never look back, and be His voice called by Him to our mother—make us all proud. Go in peace, my brother, and know that He is sending others around you now to encourage you as you prepare to complete His calling. Good-bye my dear brother, I will see you later!"

Going Down?

No sooner had he finished speaking those words than the bottom fell out from under me as if in a supercharged turbo elevator descending faster than the speed of light.

"Oh my Lord, he's alive!" I heard Mom say. Others noticed too and were ecstatic about my return. I told Mom that I been to

Heaven visiting with Stanley. She let out a yell, "Oh, dear God, Sam, he's been to Heaven and really *was* dead!"

I said to Dad, "You were right, I was not supposed to beat you up there!" He grinned that he understood. "Did you know I would come back?"

Dad said, "Yes, I knew God had to talk to you, but He had already told me that you were not going to go to Heaven before me. I just held on knowing that first of all, you have to be 'a voice to the nations' as He called you to be, and that assignment has not been completed; and second, God told me that we had to learn how to come into the 'power of agreement of prayer,' and it was that unity and agreement in prayer, Son, that brought you back here today!"

Wow, I was about to lift off again after that double affirmation. Yes, God, You do keep Your word!

There was such a tremendous difference between the light floating feeling I experienced and the weight and heaviness in my body after I returned from Heaven. I was still very weak, and felt as if I had just finished running a marathon and had just lain down to rest. I was kept in the intensive care unit under observation for a few days. My family told me that a specialist had found a blood clot in my lung—a pulmonary embolism. They had given me a form of rat poison to thin my blood. All kinds of things had been attached to me to monitor my breathing, heartbeat, etc.

My body was responding to treatment—and God's healing touch—and I was moved to a less-critical MICU room. Some of my "attachments" were removed, which made me more restful while continuing to heal; and I had more privacy, which I appreciated.

*Be not forgetful to entertain strangers: for thereby some
have entertained angels unawares* (Hebrews 13:2 KJV).

I awoke the next morning to see a man standing at the foot of
my bed. I did not ask him who he was; I was a little embar-
rassed, thinking that I probably should know him. Being in the
ministry, I have learned that people assume that pastors remember everyone they have ever met. The man smiled and said
that he was just checking on me. I thanked him. He said the
Lord gave him a word to give me.

"God says to you, John Mark Pool, that yet a little while all
the things you are familiar with will vanish, and a major shifting will begin to move you into the mandate from God. The
Lord says that you will be His voice to the nations, as He called
you by name to do. Second, the Lord says that you must tell the
people to incorporate the power of agreement in prayer and
bring His Body into the unity that Jesus prayed to Him about."

And the man paused and said, "I must go now, but remember this, too; the Lord reminds you that the enemy you were
around has been practicing witchcraft on you as a curse to kill
you. God allowed that so He could bring you to Heaven to dis-
cuss what was just spoken to you. Now you can go and accomplish His call on your life! He is going to keep you close, and
you will fulfill all that the Father has called you to do. Now be
of good cheer for He has overcome the world!" He smiled and
said, "We'll check on you later." Then he turned and walked
out of my room.

I had never seen that man before! God had sealed His word
to me so many times and in so many ways that before I was dis-
charged from the hospital, I was so fired up for Jesus that I de-
sired to see all of the nurses and staff saved! My power through
Jesus to share His Word returned, and the Lord gave me a

hunger to speak His Word. Oh, what a transformation that heavenly talk with the Father had in my life!

So far, every word has begun to be realized that I have had spoken to me. That was not only my reentry to life from physical death; it was also my reentry into the ministry after a detour onto a trail of destruction and death without God. I had turned away from my calling and what I was taught when growing up in the church. Although I was taught godly principles, it lacked the "love and the unity of the Father as the source," which I so desperately needed. It was too easy to leave behind all the religious rules and follow the wide-open detour that led to devastation and destruction. Those times were tough, but I know now that traveling that path prepared me to handle future tough circumstances and help others through trying times. All these experiences make the journey to becoming worth it.

Going Up?

This was just the beginning of the new life in the prophetic sojourn. God saw fit to allow me to die so I could cast off the effects of bad teaching that were clinging to me. I was not resurrected into perfection when I returned to earth. I was still very human in this body of flesh that must be kept under constant subjection. Yet this body of flesh is the package that God has chosen to use as a vessel to carry His Word to hurting people. Many mortals have experienced Heaven, but not all were afforded the opportunity to return to earth and make their lives right.

I am grateful that God has privileged me to share my bizarre life journey with you. My hope is that when you read about my mistakes and recognize the tough spots I faced, you will more ably maneuver around similar difficulties. I hope you learn to avoid the pitfalls along your journey. God wants me to be a voice and witnesses for you to know by my example—the good, bad, and ugly—that you do not have to live a life of destruction in order to be His voice for accountable, prophetic instruction.

I prayed fervently for the Lord to remove anything and everything from my life that was hindering my calling to complete His destiny and plans for me. I had no idea that what was about to happen next would forever strip me of all I had—bringing me to the place God needed me to be to use me for His purpose.

CHAPTER 4

Devastation

Headed out of Baton Rouge toward New Orleans, I was driving on the inside fast lane of Interstate Highway 10 West. I was on my way to minister at a large church and was looking forward to imparting into the people—by way of the power of God—all that God had given to me. During this season of my life—post-death experience—I was very focused on doing the will of God. I was so determined to fulfill the mandate of God on my life that I had stepped out in faith to walk in full-time ministry. As I was reflecting on all of these things, I heard the Lord speak in that "knowing voice" in my inner man. He said, "Turn right and go home."

"But Lord, I am going to a large church in New Orleans and am nearly there."

The voice grew more intense, "Go home!"

Immediately, I turned the steering wheel to the right as I gave way to God's instructions. All of a sudden I heard screeching brakes, honking horns, screaming citizens, and I realized how a salmon swimming upstream must feel! Here I was, a crazy man from Texas blasting across six lanes of interstate highway! I *could* have driven a little farther and pulled off at the next exit, avoiding all the demolition derby antics! However, when I got God's message, I thought it best to turn right *immediately*! For some odd reason during all the mayhem, I remembered my mother's maiden name was "Lane!" Thanks; Lord, for the "right lane." I pulled myself together and maneuvered the car back into traffic—heading back toward Texas. *Why?*

"Lord, this is a long trip, and I was so close to ministering at another great spiritual meeting. This is what I do, Lord." I kept trying to explain that it did not make sense for me to miss the meeting. My explanations did not work. He began to minister into my spirit, and as I drove the long drive home, I thought about all the blessings He had given to me throughout my life and how He had never let me down—like getting me safely over to the "right lane." I was at the point in my life when I wanted to be obedient to Him and do whatever the Father told me to do—nothing more and nothing less. This was the beginning of a turn in my life that proved it was God who destined me to make it into the "right lane."

My life, at that point, was neatly laid out—as if it were a finely set dining room table, with everything in its place. Then "someone" came along and jerked the tablecloth out from under everything. That is how I describe *devastation*. For some, devastation enters their lives when they experience the premature death of a loved one, the sudden disappearance of someone close, or the complete failure of peers in leadership. Although I had counseled and consoled many people going through devastating times, my reaction to devastation in my life was different from the way I thought I would handle it.

What Happened?

Obeying God, I was driving from the southern coastal region of the country back to my suburban home about three hours away from everything metro. I can still remember the thoughts that hung over my spirit as I finally drove into my familiar neighborhood. You know the setting, a comfortable, middle-class town anywhere in the United States. Oversized wooden-fenced lots, four-bedroom split-level homes with real-wood burning fireplaces, and two-car garages with automatic door openers. That was home to me and my family.

That day I was returning from a long and taxing ministry trip that God told me to cut short. I was rounding the last curve and caught my first glimpse of our home when I realized how tired I was and how much I needed to relax.

As I hit the garage door button and the door opened, I was happy to see the messy garage was finally cleaned! Yes, it was nice to be back home again. I retrieved my suitcase from the trunk and wearily walked to the door. Inserting the key, I felt the cold chill of lingering winter air mixed with early spring.

When I opened the door, an ocean of emptiness greeted me. Empty. No family, no furniture. I doubled over as if being hit close range in the gut with a double-barrel shotgun. In the old movies an outlaw would shoot his victim in the stomach and as he doubled over, the outlaw rode off taking his victim's horse and be-longings. The victim was "gut shot" and left to die a horribly slow death out in the desert without any water. That's how I felt.

My mind and the reality of what had happened were at odds. I walked around like a zombie just staring—at nothing. I kept wondering, *Where did everything go? It's all a big joke! Sure, that is what it is. She has moved all the junk out, put most of it in storage and then left most of the bedrooms the same and had planned on my coming home to all new stuff! Yes, I must have caught her red-handed!*

But when I went into the bedrooms, they were empty too. All of the children's belongings were gone. Finally it began to sink into my consciousness what happened. *No, I refuse to believe that sort of devil talk! I am a man of God and she is a pastor's wife. This could not be happening!* Denial of reality attacked my normal thought patterns in the mix of the emotions, with me grappling for anything to give a reason for the obvious obliteration. *Maybe she found that new place we had talked about for so long. Yes, that's it! She has moved everything and now I am going to get a call or a note saying, "Please drive to Happy Lane and see your new home!"*

Gradually, reality took hold of me. When my mind caught up with the "gut shot" of the situation, I doubled over again, this time feeling completely devastated. This was real. Only the shell of the house remained. It was not a joke. A joke was hiding a new puppy in the backyard. A joke was hiding your old easy chair until you got a new one for Father's Day. No, this was no joke. I was absolutely devastated.

I slumped down on the wide-open sea of carpet in the den and began to cry. As the magnitude of reality overwhelmed me, the pain of rejection ravaged my heart, causing me to erupt into uncontrollable sobs. I knew I was abandoned, and I knew it was for real. How could this be happening to me now? Oh, sure, I was tough to live with. Sure, we had our regular difficulties, but there was never any discussion about separating. Now everybody was gone and no matter what thoughts I tossed around in my head, it all came down to me lying on the floor in a den of desolation!

The devil kept laughing in my ear as I heard him say, "What a loser! You are not only a poor husband, a bad dad, but you're a for sure loser of a minister, too! It's over for the preaching rover! You have just seen how your 'church lifestyle' has rewarded your efforts!"

Wow! My body was numb. I lay on the floor for hours and ached. There was one old used bed in the lower level room so I crashed on it and fell into a fitful sleep.

I awoke to the fact that it wasn't a dream! I stared at the emptiness, remembering that only a few weeks ago our country home was filled with the warmth and settings of family and friends. We had enjoyed Christmas together here—birthdays and everyday living. Now I was "gut shot" again and slowly dying a horrible death.

For three days I begged God for answers. Then the devil started whispering in my ear again, "Why don't you go to the nearest liquor store and get a gallon of whiskey and a 3-liter cola and just forget about what the folks dealt you!"

LEAN ON ME

I immediately stood up and asked God for more strength. Next, I got plain old angry! Angry with myself and angry at the devil, I rummaged around and found an old folding card table and a rickety wooden chair. I set up the table in the den, put an old phone on it, retrieved my faithful preacher's Bible, and placed it on the table beside the phone.

Then I declared to the devil, "This ministry office is OPEN and will *stay open* until I leave, or God comes and takes me home!" The devil responded, "You won't be able to minister even to a sick animal! You're a loser without a family, and your church won't support you, Mr. Preacher!"

Without hesitation, I grabbed my Bible, held it up in the air, and demanded that the devil repay me seven times greater than anything he stole; and I vowed I would preach the Gospel to every nation on the earth, even if I had to be translated there by God Himself. "So, take that devil!"

It was going to be a fight to the finish line. Because I had no warning to plan for this battle, I trusted God to help me every step of the way. It was a moment-by-moment strategy that only God could lead me through.

As I sat at my "ministry office desk," the Lord told me not to lean on my own understanding, but to lean on Him in every way now, and He would direct my path. Yes! That was refreshing, and one word at a time came into my spirit while pondering what to do next.

Utilities! The word popped into my mind. I thanked the Lord that I had electricity and water. It dawned on me to call the utility companies and find out about our accounts.

"Sir, we show your account has changed to another address. The electric service to your present address is due to be cut off this afternoon."

What? Cut off my lights? "No, ma'am, please don't do that. There has been a mistake. I know we paid our electric bill for this present address," I quickly replied.

"I'm sorry, sir, but the Mrs. has ordered it."

After an hour on the phone with the utility companies, I had things settled and would not have the added devastation of being in the dark with no running water. I'm afraid living in the dark with no water would have been too much for me to handle that week. I wondered and prayed about what to do next.

Where was my family? Was my wife angry? Did she move in with her mom? Did they move out of the city, the state? I called the utility company again, and someone there gave me the new address. At least I knew they did not leave the area; they were living in a nearby city. I decided to visit her in the morning, reason with her, and by the end of the week, we'd all be together again. Wrong! Very Wrong!

When I arrived, my daughters were allowed to come outside the apartment to see Daddy. They both held me and cried. They apologized and tried to explain that they did not want to abandon me. I hugged them and asked them what happened. Their mother had another man in her life, and I quickly realized that the situation was not going to be corrected in a week—most likely never. I saw the other man in the apartment as the girls went inside. As the door closed, I felt a death nail pound into my heart. Accepting the facts was too hard, especially since there was no warning, no discussion. I shuffled back to the car realizing that I was one of millions of Americans who go through the heartache of separation and divorce. What does a person do who loses his wife, children, home, and pastoral office?

Pastoral office...? Yes, that's it—the pastoral office! Oddly enough, while survival instincts and questions raged through my mind, I had not even considered seeking the assistance of my senior pastor. As I drove "home," I was busy wondering where to go and what to do next when my answer was just two miles down the road.

I was an associate pastor at a local church and the senior pastor there was like a brother and friend to me. This man had helped me with previous problems, but I did not know how to talk to him about being "thrown over a cliff!" Leaders who are reading this now, think about that sobering thought. I struggled to find words to adequately depict my plight.

How could I talk about total devastation that affected not only my family, but also the lives of all the people who were involved in my ministry? Although I was certain I was called by God to bring His Word to the nations, I felt like a total loser. Part of me was convinced that the anointing of God rested heavily on my life, while the other part of me felt like a car that was "totaled" in a horrific accident. The truth is, I felt like I was dying—not physically as before; now I was dying spiritually and emotionally.

As I tried to put the pieces of my life back together, along the way I lost my motivation, my drive. I fell into an agony of uselessness—any attempt at normalcy seemed futile. I was quickly approaching a "danger zone" from which many do not survive! I survived only by the grace of God and many prayers of those who cared for my life and calling. In this zone, the enemy of our souls tries to persuade us that it is time for us to "end it"— to snuff out the life that God gave us. God can deliver us from the devil's assignment of death if we trust in Jesus!

DANCING WITH THE DEVIL

I learned that if I allowed the enemy to talk me out of seeking the right help, godly help, I was delaying healing. By the "right" help, I do not mean going to my friend who lives a "clean respectable" life, yet does not know the Lord Jesus Christ as his Savior. Many seek solace in unsafe sanctums. It is not a good thing to go to a person who appears to have it together and yet does not have an eternal perspective of the Kingdom of God!

Be careful that you don't throw kerosene on a smoldering fire. Kerosene is not as combustible as gasoline, so it doesn't ignite immediately—it might even seem to stop the smoldering.

However, deep inside is that one unresolved ember left over from a once raging fire. The dormant ember is like an undetected disease that left unattended will explode into something deadly. The "good intentions" of dousing a fire with kerosene may help initially, but eventually it erupts into an even deadlier raging fire. Seeking help from someone who looks right and has good intentions will not solve the problem in the long run—seek godly advice.

Beware; the enemy will be very near, and he has been given legal access by the choices we made when we did not obey God when the problem first surfaced. We give the enemy additional license to destroy us because of the wrong counsel we sought. The devil hopes we will continue to seek company for our misery, so he can keep hosing the fire with more kerosene! He will not let us alone until we get to the root of our sin and repent. Dancing with the devil and his kind will guarantee our eternal destruction.

This isn't about drinking alcohol or taking drugs—it's about dealing with the deep down sin. It would be easy if all we had to do was "just say no!" Saying "no" only postpones our lifeless time on this earth until we have to deal with it in His eternal Kingdom. Rest assured, each of us will deal with what is inside on that final day of accounting for our spirits that were created to bring glory to the King. If the outward signs were the issue, we could say the person who has never eaten any type of harmful food is an outstanding person. Yet, it is not what goes in, but what comes out of us that proves the issues of our hearts. Jesus Christ said:

> *"Don't you understand either?" he asked. "Can't you see that the food you put into your body cannot defile you? Food doesn't go into your heart, but only passes through the stomach and then goes into the sewer." (By saying this, He*

*declared that every kind of food is acceptable in God's eyes.)
And then he added, "It is what comes from inside that de-
files you. For from within, out of a person's heart, come evil
thoughts, sexual immorality, theft, murder, adultery, greed,
wickedness, deceit, lustful desires, envy, slander, pride, and
foolishness. All these vile things come from within; they are
what defile you"* (Mark 7:18-23 NLT).

HOPE COMPLETION CENTERS

So what do you do with those smoldering embers inside
you? I suggest you go to a trusted person who knows Jesus as
his personal Savior and who has a record of accomplishment
dealing with and healing broken lives. After all the devastation
I had been through, helping people—especially pastors and
leaders—through brokenness has become one of my passions.

In the future I hope to open healing centers for those who are
desperate for a turnaround in their lives—people who think
there are no solutions for them. As the Lord opens the doors,
my vision is to strategically position "spiritual restoration centers" in rural settings all across the United States. They will be
located in private yet safe areas where individuals will have all
the amenities of home and feel safe as they pursue private healing of their inner person.

My dream of helping devastated leaders be restored to
God's plans will become a reality. The name God gave me for
this ministry summarizes our mission: Hope Completion Cen-
ters™— *where hearts are mended, souls are secured, and lives are
restored!*©

God was serious about changing lives when He sent His son
Jesus Christ to come to His created earth both for the purpose
of restoring His creation to its rightful position with Him, and

for providing eternal life in His Kingdom! I thank Him for the opportunity He has given me to help build His Kingdom on earth as it is in Heaven!

FROM DEVASTATION TO DEPRESSION

My folks lived through the "Great Depression," and we heard about the tough times—many times throughout the years. Living through the Depression era required rigid discipline to make a sustainable lifestyle on very little disposable income. As most households in the 1950s, our large family was supported by only one income. We made as many creative adjustments as possible to get by each month. People today call it "penny-pinching."

In those days, if the sole "breadwinner" lost a job, it caused even more post-Depression economic consequences. Finding and keeping a job was paramount to families who lived either during or after the Great Depression. These people knew how to be wise stewards of their income. My parents frequently gave us this history lesson hoping we would avoid "being without."

Learning how to be a good steward and how to adjust during hard times were not the only lessons that I learned from my parents. I also learned that devastation isn't confined to failed marriages and financial ruin. In reality, you can be devastated by anything you consider an answer which turns out to be totally false. Being devastated by broken promises, dreams, or hopes lead to depression. People instinctively use coping mechanisms that lower their levels of stress. They find ways to alleviate the constant pain of abiding loss that resides in a lower level of the conscious mind. Thus, subconsciously, many of these people—I venture to say most—are operating daily in "manageable depression."

Depression affects both Christians and non-Christians alike. Although it is not as pronounced in the Christian lifestyle, it becomes obvious when we uncover in whom or what we place our trust. Most people do not receive proper training in how to build their lives on the solid bedrock foundation of the Kingdom of God. If we really believe what the Bible says—and not what others tell us—we can survive any storm in life. The enemy has an easy way with most Christians, because pride comprises too much of their foundation. They have built a "false sense of spiritual perfection from pride," and then they are not able to handle setbacks.

During this time of devastation, any pride I had was completely lost. Pride is dangerous because it prevents us from admitting mistakes and facing problems head on. We don't want to "lose face" in our peer groups or in front of our family. For those three days after walking into my empty house, I "checked out" of reality. Fortunately, I was not suicidal—the ultimate goal of our adversary, the devil. I was devastated and saddened, but I knew I was never going to stop doing what God called me to do.

The enemy uses depression as a weapon of death. He keeps his weapon loaded and throws troubles in your way, allowing you to fall deeper and deeper into yourself so you believe there is no hope and no way out. He hands you the loaded weapon while you are playing "spiritual roulette." He gives sedatives, excuses, false friends, and many other ingredients to keep you dependent on him or yourself and too frantic to look to your one true Counselor. Don't fall for it! Through the tears and pain, I thought back to my meeting in Heaven and the mandate from God on my life. I read Scripture aloud and determined to do and say what God said. Bible in hand, I got mad at the devil and continually decreed God's victory in my life.

It took our country years to recover from the Great Depression, but the country, like most people, began to forget about the hard times and hard labor when thoughts shifted to the war raging in Europe. At my age, I knew the liberty of an extended recovery time was not an option; I wondered though, if I would ever be able to forget all the battles taking place in my life. Life takes us from one event to another while we push the entire base of our reason farther away from the solution—the Kingdom of God! Apart from God, there is no solid base. All other ground is shifting sand.

Weigh the Cost

My parents told me the one thing they both learned about going through the Great Depression period was how to "weigh the cost" associated with anything of value. When they were "dirt poor," before they let go of a penny, they "weighed the cost to the value of 'do I really need it?'" I believe that way of thinking has escaped our "baby boomer" generation. We would do well to take the best values of that earlier era and adapt them into our spiritual lifestyles. I do not in the least advocate a "poverty spirit" mentality—the one that came with living in the eccentric flesh and hoarding every dime. Quite the contrary.

Although my parents were not wealthy, they were givers. They actually gave more than I see given in many churches today. It was not always money they had to give—and they gave plenty of that—but an attitude of sowing all of their lives into the Body of Christ. If that meant chopping a cord of firewood for the preacher's house, or making dinner (from "scratch" not from the deli) for a church social or for a grieving family, then that's what they did. They mowed grass for widows and painted houses for invalids—no charge. That is a spirit of giving. When my parents made money, they could put it through a "wringer washer" and double the buying power.

That is not a poverty spirit; rather, it is an attitude of accountability for what God entrusted to you. We in the "boomer bunch" must fight to put the right attitude and perspective about giving back into the church and our families where it belongs.

When we face hard times—and we all will—our perspective will either give us hope or cause severe depression because we have no hope. With God as our source and with a resolve that no matter the battle we are assured that God will get us through victoriously; we can all have hope! We can see every situation with a hopeful perspective when we live as citizens of His Kingdom.

However, when we are being bombarded from all sides and feel ourselves slipping, even though we know that God is our source, we need to seek professional and accountable spiritual support. During the heavy-duty attacks, get help that will be honest and loving. This is no time to allow "Job's friends—the judgmental jury" to offer more fuel for your fires. We all experience personal attacks, but regional and national attacks readjust our values and perspective for God's creation. Being with God doesn't give us total insulation from the devastations of life. However, He does give us a way to escape the world's shaking and realigning of priorities.

When we begin to weigh the cost of living for God, it becomes obvious that the rewards of His blessing are increased as we become more obedient, which is better than any sacrifice. To hear Him and to obey Him is always better than the former desires that provided only temporal comforts. God is for real; He loves you; and He hurts when you hurt. He pursues your presence more than you are pursuing His. You are of great value to Him—He weighed the cost, and sent His Son to die for you.

Mt. Carmel

After I saw my daughters, I made sure the utilities and the empty house were secured. Then God impressed on me to stay inside for a few days to seek His counsel. My ministry calendar came to mind and I realized that I had a morning and evening service scheduled for the upcoming Sunday. I said, "God, I just can't do this!"

God responded speaking to my spirit, "You must go; it is your Mt. Carmel." I knew that Mt. Carmel is where the prophet Elijah had a showdown with Jezebel's Baal priests. I knew that God meant that I must go to Dallas and follow through with my commitment. After unsuccessfully pleading my case not to go, I climbed into my van. As I drove, I felt as if a double case of influenza had consumed my body. Picking up my cell phone, I tried to call the pastor. I was going to kindly explain that I had the flu and needed to bow out of my commitment to speak in Dallas. Each time I punched in his number, the call would not go through. Nearing my destination, I asked God what I should do when the pastor comes out of his house and asks where my family is. God clearly spoke to me, "Just tell him they stayed home." It happened exactly the way I had just seen it in my mind. The pastor walked out of the house and immediately asked, "Where are the wife and kids?" I said, "They stayed home this trip."

He invited me to stay at his home rather than pay for a hotel room. That was ordained of God. He and his wife treated me like an adopted son. My sickness got worse, and as it did, it became apparent that I was going to lose my voice. The pastor told me that he would be glad to go ahead and preach if I was too sick. Not knowing where or how this happened, a "knowing burst of faith" arose within me and I declared, "Pastor, if you have to carry me up to that pulpit and hold the microphone near my mouth, I am going to give the Word of the Lord tomorrow!" He laughed and said, "I like your faith, son!" That night I slept more soundly than I had during the entire past "week of wreckage."

Upon awakening for the Sunday service at "Mt. Carmel," I was so choked up and felt so ill that I placed my Bible on my body and demanded the body to line up with the Word of God. That, plus the extremely hot shower and the dogged determination that was coming from what was now an "angry faith," pushed me forward. As I started up to the pulpit to preach, I could not talk above a hoarse whisper. But as soon as I held the microphone and began praising God, the Anointing of the Holy Spirit hit me, and my voice was clear and strong! The service was God-ordained, and we had every form of inner hurts healed in the morning service.

Upon returning to the pastor's home, I was relieved to rest again and was about to take a much needed nap when the Lord nudged me and told me to change my evening sermon to "healing." As I was arguing to keep my nap appointment, God asked if I wanted to speak again! I tried to talk, but I had lost my voice completely! In my thoughts I replied, *"Yes, Lord, whatever you want; you know I am going to do it!"* I stayed up all afternoon and wrote out the entire new message on healing. When I was back on the platform and the microphone was back in hand, we began to lift up the name of Jesus Christ and my voice was crystal clear.

The message was titled, "There is a Healer in the House." We had a week's revival that day and many people were totally healed and delivered from every form of sickness and disease.

God totally healed my body of sickness and I had no more flu symptoms. No, it was not my feelings that caused this great out-pouring, it was strictly an act of faith in His Word and making myself obey. That was my Mt. Carmel—God was preparing me to walk with Him along the pathway of the prophetic sojourn that was stretching out in front of me.

Paying the Price

I was scheduled to attend a pastor's conference in Oklahoma, so I thanked the pastor and his wife for their hospitality and drove toward Oklahoma. I had been praying that entire week for God to show me what was going to happen to the family I had lost. He reminded me that I had walked through my house a couple of months earlier and anointed every room with oil. I had declared that anything in my home, family, or life that wasn't of God or would not be able to follow Him with obedience was to get out.

"Yes Lord, but this could not mean losing an entire family, could it?" God replied, "Only if they will not make a choice to follow in my calling obediently." Wow! I never thought about what had happened quite like that. I never thought God would clean an entire family off my plate! God reminded me that all humans have a choice to make. We can choose to follow His calling and destiny for us and reap both earthly and eternal blessings, or we can choose not to obey His will for us and stumble through life without His love and peace.

I listened to God as I drove the few hours to the conference. The Lord said into my spirit man that He was about to adjust me into my "prophetic calling of destiny" that had not been allowed up to that point in my life. I asked Him why not until now, and He replied into my heart that I was not paying the price to obey, and others were not either, as they would have to line up or it would destroy the man in the mantle. This began to make sense, yet I had many questions and for sure wanted to know something about the immediate future. When I arrived at the hotel, I prayed earnestly and was in a very diligent soul-searching mode.

The Lord began to speak more clearly than I had ever heard Him speak to me before. Hearing His voice was like talking to someone who is sitting next to you or spending time with your closest friend or brother—all day, every day. I asked Him how to tell my senior pastor (at the church where I was serving as an associate pastor and missions director) about my recent devastation. I kept hearing from God to wait 30 days. I was obedient, and the timing of God during the next month proved to be extremely and critically important.

INSTRUCTION AND DESTRUCTION

As I drove into the church parking lot for the pastor's conference, I had a sinking feeling hit me as if I did not belong there. I shrugged it off and walked into the building full of leaders and pastors. Then the voice of God told me to walk straight out of there and go back to my car. "Lord," I said while walking to the car, "is the conference a bad deal?"

"No, it is *their* deal—not yours! Now go to your hotel, check out, and head straight south on I-35 toward Dallas." His direction was as clear as if I was hearing someone talking aloud to me; I found peace with each new step of obedience. I did as I was told, and the person at the hotel front desk asked if there was an emergency. I explained there was and I must immediately head to Dallas. Thankfully, she did not charge me for the additional nights I had reserved.

During my drive south, I paid close attention to the highway near Denton, Texas. As I drove, the Lord told me to pull off at a certain location and a certain exit. I had never been there before, and by then it was late evening. The Lord instructed me to go to the right and check into a local hotel directly in front of me. I did that and asked God what I was doing there. I was not really tired; I knew no one in the area; and I wondered why God told me to stop. As I was again praying in my hotel room, the Lord told me to get some clothes ironed and get ready to preach tomorrow night in Dallas.

"Lord, I don't mean to question you, as this is really getting to be fun, but could You fill me in a little more on why I stopped here if Dallas is only an hour or so south of where I am now?"

God said, "Open the phone book and look up churches. Find the one with My Glory on it. I am connecting you with Zion."

Wow! I was very curious now. I looked in the Denton phone book, and sure enough, there was in the church section: *Glory of Zion Church*. The Lord told me to get up in the morning and go to the church and meet the people. He said, "I am connecting you with a company of prophets."

"You mean in this modern day there are companies of prophets?" I asked the Lord. "You have no idea," God mused with me! Are you holding onto your chair yet? I located the church on the map and wrote down the directions. The hotel God directed me to was within walking distance of the church! Sure enough, the next morning I walked into the shopping center church office and asked if I could speak with the director of the company of prophets. She smiled and said, "Oh, are you here to see Prophet Chuck Pierce?"

"Sure," I said, "if he is the director of the company of prophets." She let me know that he would qualify as that. Then she said that Chuck and the local pastor, Robert Heidler, were in Colorado together for a meeting that day. But the "prophetic praise leader," John Dixon, was available to meet me for a few minutes. I had never heard of a prophetic praise leader, but I told her I would be glad to meet with any "pastor." Mr. Dixon greeted me with all the smiles and warmth of a very loving and genuine man of God. He kindly invited me into his office and asked me what he could do for me.

"God told me to stop and meet a group of leaders at a place called 'Glory' and that it had a company of prophets here," I said.

He smiled and said God was right, but they were not in the office. He invited me to return on Sunday for church services and I could meet them then. He knew I had been dealing with some heart issues—I could sense it by the way he treated me. Mr. Dixon then asked if he could pray with me. I welcomed the offer, and we had a good prayer time. It touched my heart deeply, as he had no earthly idea what I had been through the past couple of weeks. As I was leaving, he hugged my neck and offered me a free copy of his new CD of praise and worship to take along. I accepted his gift, and I still listen to the "Roar of the Lion" as God used many of those songs to minister to me mightily along the journey.

I received a call when back on the road headed to Dallas in obedience to the next unknown assignment God had for me. "Pastor Leland Hall here." It was the pastor of the church where I had ministered last week during my Mt. Carmel experience—the service that was full of God's glory. "Fellow, what are you doing?"

"I'm driving down south on I-35 coming out of Denton, Texas," I told him.

"Why don't you come by to see me here in Grand Prairie, and if you don't have a service scheduled, would you preach for me Wednesday night?"

"Oh, sure, I'd love that!" I quickly secured the date. He asked why I was not at the pastor's conference in Oklahoma and I told him that God had re-routed me. I explained that God had instructed me to go to a Glory of Zion church in Denton. Pastor Hall knew about a well-known prophet there by the name of Chuck Pierce. He asked if I met him. I explained what had happened and told him about my initial steps to connect with the anointing that was there.

Pastor Hall invited me to dinner, and I accepted. The Lord told me to tell Pastor Hall about what happened to me, the empty house, the week of devastation, the day of destruction when I saw my wife in an apartment with another man. I argued in my spirit, thinking the pastor would immediately cancel my Wednesday night service that we just scheduled. But finally I said to God, "Oh well, OK, OK, why not just get it all out in the open, that way I will feel much better about not holding back the truth about what I've been going through."

As we sat at the table after finishing our meal, I told Pastor Hall and his wife, Glenda, all the sad details. I did not even know it, but tears were streaming down my face. Here I was with a man who was not showing anger, pity, or disgust; instead, his eyes were glowing with love, acceptance, and forgiveness.

"Well, son, you don't have to worry about a thing with me. I have been through the same thing in my background in the ministry, and you were put here by God's divine assignment to get some help."

By that time I was joyfully numb and wondering what else God had up His sleeve. Oh, it only gets better on the path to becoming a prophet.

CHAPTER 5

Correction Course

GOD ADJUSTS REALITY

When searching for explanations, we sometimes look into the lives of those near us who are going through a series of battles, and wonder what sin is in their camp that is causing such continual destruction.

The conversation between the disciples and Jesus about the sin and the person born blind comes to mind:

And His disciples asked Him, saying, "Rabbi, who sinned, this man or his parents, that he was born blind?" Jesus answered, "Neither this man nor his parents sinned, but that the works of God should be revealed in him" (John 9:2,3 NKJV).

Understanding came to me that sin and disobedience result in consequences that God determines. All decisions to obey or disobey

Him are accompanied by consequences. The consequences are determined by our decisions about whom we are going to serve.

The journey along this exciting adventure gradually increased the number of decisions I had to make regarding my future. One immediate decision was made in obedience to go to Denton and Dallas. I stayed over and became well acquainted with Pastors Leland and Glenda Hall at Victory Temple Church in Grand Prairie, Texas. Glenda went to Lubbock to visit her children which gave Pastor Hall and me a God-ordained time to get better acquainted. After our ministry schedule together, we talked about my future plans. "I really don't know what to do now," I told him.

"Why don't you go back home and check on things there, visit with your mother, and then pray about coming back here and working with me for a season as my associate pastor."

I thought I was hearing a message directly from God sitting on His throne!

"But don't you realize that my life is basically gutted? How could you possibly be asking *me* to come and work for you as an associate pastor?"

"That is exactly what I am asking you to do," Pastor Hall said.

I took his advice and headed back to see if my marriage could be saved and our family restored. As I drove home, I heard the Lord tell me to send an e-mail to my wife and let her know that God was giving us a chance to repent and reconcile.

That evening as I returned to my very cold, dark, empty house, I realized that God was either going to bring them back home, or He would move me forward toward His destiny for me. Remaining in this environment of devastation offered too much opportunity for battles with depression. It was too easy to visualize "the way life used to be." Choosing a change of scenery does not necessarily mean I was running from the battle. No, I was listening carefully to God, as everyone should who is in the midst of a battle, because He may be preparing you for the best blessings you have ever known.

There is a time and season for everything under the sun. *"To every thing there is a season, and a time to every purpose under the heaven"* (Eccles. 3:1 KJV).

The children of God are not accidents placed on an insignificant place called earth among millions of other galaxies. God has uniquely constructed this world so that a billion different events will come and go exactly on His schedule. He offers us opportunities to find happiness or sorrow, as we understand the importance of choosing His path for our lives. God did not make a random world void of significance. He created one that offers opportunities at various intervals throughout our years, months, days, and moments. The world God created has a well-balanced arrangement. Nothing is left to chance in God's world. Our Creator, and yet very personal Father, holds everything in His judicious and omnipotent hand. He is a very wise and caring God.

I learned along my path that you would do well to bear that truth in mind during your battles. You are not left to mere chance on a scientific cosmos devoid of intricate and divine providence. You are not an accident waiting to happen.

Blind fate is a terrible comfort in following a creator. How comforting it is for us to know that the proceedings of the universe are well thought out by a concerned, gracious, loving, and faithful God. When tragedy or disappointment strikes, those who believe in God's love have only to wait patiently for the hour of deliverance that will surely come. Your day of restoration will come as you learn to place all your trust in your Father. Our Father who is in Heaven, also by our decision to abide with Him, is affecting our Kingdom that is then and now coming to be in this earth—just as it is in Heaven. That is a powerful revelation for us to realize.

Blind fate is how the world instructs its own to address the day of destruction—a horrible consolation during tragedy. It is such a comfort to know, that no matter the fault, the reason, or the cause, God is more compassionate than we will ever realize until we sit at His feet in Heaven one day and He opens our minds completely. He is very long-suffering, and He is a faithful God. Remember to turn to your loving Father when—not if—the battle in your life rages. Even if you do not immediately see or experience His presence because of your despair, *do not give up!* Do not fold in the midst of the battle! Keep looking to the Lord; He knows how much you can handle, and He will never give you more than you can bear.

Also, if you do not grow weary, and if you do not turn from Him, yet stay the course and honestly wait upon Him, then believe me, believe many biblical examples, and believe hundreds of testimonies of change, that God will bring you an "hour of redemption." The breakthrough Master is about to breakthrough for you!

No Recourse

During prayer while sitting at my computer, I clearly heard the Lord again instruct me to send my wife an e-mail to warn her of the required sacrifice for disobedience. I wrote to her that in 30 days, unless she repented, returned home, and committed to restoring our marriage, God would require a great price for her decision. The essence of the message I believe God prompted me to write was a warning that she had left His anointed protection.

I asked her to consider wisely the decisions she made to alter my prophetic voice and that no one should harm God's anointed or His prophets.

I received her e-mail response the next day. The summary of her reply suggested that I contact her again only through an attorney. She wrote that she had moved into an apartment, had filed for a divorce, and was going on with her life. She wrote that my "scare and fear" tactics were not going to make her change her mind.

When I read her reply, although my mind would not hear it, the desires of my heart for reconciliation were shattered in the natural. Not only did my heart feel broken, but the worst part was an *ominous and foreboding* feeling that hit me deep in the pit of my stomach. This has rarely happened to me, but each time it has left me feeling very nauseated. As I read her reply, I felt as if I was going to vomit—not because I was angry or in retaliation—it was a sickness that made me hurt in empathy for her, knowing that she made a bad choice, and knowing the consequences would be severe.

At my mother's suggestion, I moved into her home as she had recently relocated to a full-care nursing facility. This was another *God moment* during my sojourn that allowed a safe, temporary transitional location for me. Furthermore, it was left up to me to sell our home and tie up all the loose ends from our years of marriage and family life. After that, I was ready for whatever God had in mind for me. Most of this time of transition is a blur in my mind, as I gasped for the breadth of meaning and consolation from God. None of what I was going through seemed right.

With a staging area complete, God indeed opened the door, and I moved to Grand Prairie, Texas, and accepted the "healing assignment" offered by my "ravens at the Brook Cherith." I likened this time to when the prophet Elijah experienced some of his greatest tests and victories atop Mt. Carmel.

> *And the word of the Lord came unto him, saying, Get thee hence, and turn thee eastward, and hide thyself by the brook Cherith, that is before Jordan. And it shall be, that thou shalt drink of the brook; and I have commanded the ravens to feed thee there* (1 Kings 17:2-4 KJV).

A Hiding Place With God

Victory Temple took me in as a "long lost son." I received the love and warmth of a prodigal son coming home to a family that knew exactly what I needed. I had been so devastated that I had forgotten what it was like to be really loved. Their love was so warm it almost scared me deep inside. I adjusted quickly and quite well and began to feel newness of life deep in my aching veins. The Lord provided a house for me to lease that was located on the next street over from my pastor's home. I frequently walked over to his home for fellowship in the morning.

This environment and ministry was far better than I could have ever hoped or dreamed of, considering my recent overnight transformation from family man and local minister to complete abandonment and total submission to hearing and obeying the voice of God. As Pastor Leland and Glenda nurtured my heart and took me in like a wounded animal left to die, they knew more than I of the many dangers waiting just below the surface of my new lifestyle.

As I pieced together things that I needed to make my new home habitable and completed settling things at my former house, I traveled back and forth frequently. It was about a three-hour drive from the "destruction zone" to my new place. I was never one to run from my problems, yet this was a most comforting change. New places with new faces made a world of difference. The family at my new church pulled together and held an old-fashioned "pounding" to make sure I had dishes, utensils, and the necessary items to set up housekeeping as a soon-to-be single parent.

I was planning to return to my mother's house immediately after the Sunday morning service to pick up a few more personal belongings. As I walked out to the doorway, shook parishioners' hands and hugged them good-bye for the week, a group invited me to a favorite Mexican restaurant. I tried to excuse myself from this overabundance of kind hospitality, but the pastor and close associates would not take "no" as an answer.

We drove to the restaurant and when I was getting out of my car, my new church family circled around me and asked me to sit down, because there was something I needed to know. The pastor looked painfully into my eyes and said, "Your former pastor and friend called this morning and said he was trying to contact you today to inform you that your stepson was killed last night in a car accident." I sat there stunned. It was my second wife's only son. I began to cry as this new shock jarred my already mangled and tangled emotions. These wonderful people formed a close circle around me, knowing much of what had brought me to them just a few short weeks ago.

Then I realized it was the end of the month that God had told me to e-mail the warning to my wife. What a mess this was turning out to be. The more I prayed and stood on faith, the worse things looked in the natural. But I knew God was being faithful to keep His word. Then a false sense of hope appeared, and I thought that maybe this destruction in her life would make her come back to me. But no, she did not want to see or talk to me.

It was a very difficult setting, because I had not told my former church pastor or members that my family left me. The Lord had told me to wait for a month before explaining things to my former pastor. By then he certainly knew about the separation and now it would be awkward and different from the way I had envisioned in my spirit to tell him. Because he didn't know, members of my former church were trying to deliver cards, food, and condolences to our former home—now vacant.

God reminded me of the date and the e-mail about consequences. It took a lot to shake me after having been emotionally wiped out. Catastrophe catapulted my thoughts into the future that only served as a short-term false hope. God had given His word to warn, and then God kept His word. God knows our hearts, and we are not the judges. Life continues; many times things happen that we cannot even imagine, nor can our finite minds explain them. Yet, we can choose to learn from each situation, each joy, and each tragedy. When it seems you are at the lowest level of your soul, keep your eyes focused on the Lord.

The Black Day

During that catastrophic period of destruction on top of devastation, God began to deal with me about the way I approached my assignments. When I would pray and ask God for direction, more often than not, I immediately looked around for signs to align with my expectations of how it would work. In other words, it was not a truthful waiting; rather, it became a "ritual" to coat my desires of what I wanted to happen in a spiritual sanctioning. This approach is also found in many of the "church-of-what-is-happening-now" settings. It has been taught for years by the religious ranks giving justifiable doses of "christianeeze" flavoring for proof it was a "godly decision."

God was telling me that He must be the only voice I hear, and it would only be heard through time alone with Him—and I should not confuse my own desires and designs with His directions. This was a new process for me to learn, and I realized that my future was in a chaotic transition from decisions birthed in the carnal realm. Worse than my chaos was my realization that no matter how painful the process had become, this affected many more lives than simply my own. A "domino effect" often takes place, and the lessons that are taught through the choices made were now coming home to rest.

The Lord prompted me to find out when the funeral services for my stepson were going to take place. Because of moving out of the area and my marriage situation, I was placed on the outer loop for receiving any information. I made calls to the city where the funeral was to be conducted, and was told that it was scheduled for the next day.

Although I knew attending the funeral would be extremely emotionally difficult, the Lord told me I must go on this assignment and be part of the family mixture that represented volumes of differences in relationships. I had a cousin accompany me to the funeral.

As I walked up to the memorial gardens where the funeral was about to begin, a mix of feelings were bouncing around within me on how to respond in this setting. There was my stepson's biological father, who had been on the peripherals for the past 14 plus years. Next was my estranged wife, the mother of the son being buried. Also there was my immediate family and members of our church where I had been on staff. By then it was obvious to most that my wife and I were not "together," since another man was consoling her. It was a very awkward situation.

Wanting to pay my respects, I walked up front to the registration book to sign my name.

His mother was draped in black, as were our daughters, and she appeared to be holding her breath as we stared into each other's eyes for the last time as husband and wife. As I signed my name, standing within arm's length of the front "family" row under the canopy that provided cover from the East Texas heat, I could feel death.

What happened that caused more than one life to be buried that day? It was like being in a movie, and the will was about to be read settling a large estate. All the interested and invited guests were sitting on the edge of life's chair, waiting to hear the last will and testament. Some of the interested and invited guests would be pleased with the reading—others would be disappointed or angry.

My role as guest left me empty. No matter what my faith demanded, or which Scripture was read, standing there in front of that young man's casket, screams within me shouted for peace. I needed peace to move on, peace to forgive, and peace to love. Restoration was not reborn at the memorial service. The look in her eyes told me that I would never again be part of her life. Many unresolved emotions were buried that day, as I realized that I was truly being replaced as head of the house, husband, and father. My replacement watched me intently, wondering about my presence and attitude.

COURSE CORRECTION

The scene at the funeral seemed unnatural. It was as if in my spirit man I could hear this statement being read:

Today is all for one moment in time to make a statement: *A course correction has been made* and is now on record, brought to light for all to see. The Chief Accountant has corrected the books as it is decreed. It is now publicly recorded, and so shall it be known as entered on permanent records—*course corrected*. You are free to go ahead with your lives. Your past failures and previous decisions have now been revealed by My light on both sides. You have both paid an extremely high price to have the course corrected.

God spoke to me and said, "Now walk with Me into new futures. Her future is paid for and secured in writing upon that headstone behind her. John Mark, your future was also forever etched into the minds of all those friends, family, and acquaintances for this immediate area—as you knew it before—has been publicly announced as buried, along with all idol worship and past dreams."

I thanked God for providing the revelation and my "Brook Cherith." It never looked better than the day I drove toward it and away from the increasing aroma of "fresh rumor food" dished up after the funeral.

I came to realize that God calls each of us personally. Each one of us is ultimately responsible for fulfilling the call and assignment of God on our lives. However others may feel about this concept, I am so completely convinced that I will continue following God's calling and His requirement for me to minister to the nations. That is what my assignment is now; and it will only increase. I publish books because God told me to publish His words. You are reading a portion of that message of my life as a living epistle to point you to His love, acceptance, and forgiveness.

Although I have been ordained for more than 20 years as a minister to perform weddings, administer last rites, or conduct funeral services, my primary mission is to be a prophetic voice for God.

The Father chastens those He loves. And I pray that you have learned enough from my mistakes to prevent you from committing the same. Man may impart by the laying on of hands, and he may fill out paperwork to both formally and legally establish your ability to perform religious acts, but it is God who calls you—it is only His anointing that will perform the miraculous feats that are necessary to do what He has called you to complete.

God's calls each of us individually, and we will each stand before Him and give an account for what we did with what He gave us to perform our assignments in His Kingdom. I take that responsibility extremely serious these days. For that reason, I am called upon to share much of my life as an example to equip others who need to get through those tough days along the journey. Yes, my life is a sojourn for the King. In that adventure, God highlights these words, "It is the journey that is the calling." The journey is becoming a prophet. For me, it is the sojourn He has placed me on that is the *path of becoming a prophet*.

Life Goes On

If you have ever weathered some serious storms, you can probably also attest to the fact that if you simply "stay the course," things will eventually get better. Sometimes storms go from bad to worse, but they eventually subside in God's timing. Through faith, you will stay on course and cause others to follow you on the straight and narrow path.

As time passed, I returned to as much normalcy as possible. I was concerned as the days turned to weeks that I was still in the ministry, technically still married, and a pastor living in another city. This is not a normal situation for a pastor. However, my new church family was never judgmental of me. I believe their attitude reflects a new hunger people have today for "real" pastors to come to the forefront. When there are as many divorces in the pews as on the streets, something must be done to address this issue in a very honest fashion.

One of many things I learned through all my troubles: no two people are alike, just as no two divorces are alike. After years of counseling with people, I can say positively that no matter how many family, divorce recovery, or Christian psychology authors you read, you are unique. Your marriage is (or was) unique because the two people involved are different from each other and all others.

As I mentioned in a previous chapter, please do not look for advice from "armchair quarterbacks" who never read a Bible nor enter a church door. That person is not capable of giving you godly advice. They will offer plenty of suggestions, but nothing can come close to what you will learn from God when you spend a few hours alone meditating upon Him and His love and presence. I finally learned to focus as Mary did and sit at the feet of Jesus, giving Him my time. This is one key ingredient that has saved my life.

My new life at Victory Temple was a sweet blend of giving and receiving. As Pastor Glenda told me, "We have been your love family of ravens here to nurture you back to spiritual health." I appreciated her use of the word "ravens," for ravens had saved the life of the prophet Elijah by feeding him, as related in the Old Testament. Oh, did they ever save me by feeding both my spirit and my body! They were truly "ravens" to me. My heart is where it is now because of the love, the fellowship, meals, and the unselfish gifts given to a struggling, wounded warrior. They took care of me without an expectation of return. "Ravens" will receive a blessing from sowing into my life, future, and the ministry that satan wanted to destroy. May God bless all "ravens" forever.

CHAPTER 6

Banishment

BANNED!

After being nurtured back to spiritual and emotional health at Victory Temple, I felt God calling me out and I accepted a position at a large church in a suburban community in Louisiana. My role there as pastor, prophet, and minister was exciting; I was fulfilling my calling and using my God-given talents and skills through a number of ministry areas.

My confidence was growing in my new leadership role, and I felt I was truly serving my God. I accepted expanded roles, including working on and editing a new church magazine. I was truly as happy as I could have been considering my circumstances as a lonesome single person. For these reasons, I was utterly dumbfounded when I was called into conference and given the following ultimatum: "Either completely delete that woman from your life, or get your office things packed and get out of this building and this church and do not come back, ever!

You are no longer welcome on this church property or any of our properties or locations! And in case you don't understand what you have just been told, let me tell you clearly again—if you set foot on any of our church's properties, you will be physically thrown off! Now get out of here and get your office packed, and do it right now. And make sure you move out of our member's house by the end of today!"

What?! Ousted? I was being thrown out of church? It was final and over? I was being thrown out as if a criminal convicted of a heinous crime. For some reason at that moment, I remembered reading about a man who opened fire with a semi-automatic rifle wounding and killing parishioners during a Sunday morning service. Certainly I wasn't a mass murderer—what did they think I had done?! I was bewildered and completely stunned. Death by stoning would have been an easier to accept than what I was going through.

Standing as numb as if in subzero weather, I stared in utter disbelief as the number two man in charge in of the church refused to shake my hand after the sincere apology I extended to him in love. Then he abruptly turned about face and screamed commands at the top of his lungs as he stomped out the door, slamming it so hard that all the pictures on the walls shook. I did not need discernment to tell me that we were not going to have another meeting about this. It was time to turn in my keys and start packing my personal office belongings.

I was assigned a "bodyguard" from our pastoral brigade to follow me around as a watchdog to ensure that I would not attempt any retaliation. Then God told me I would be learning a lot more about Matthew 5:44-45: *"But I say, love your enemies! Pray for those who persecute you! In that way, you will be acting as true children of your Father in Heaven. For He gives His sunlight* to both the evil and the good, and he sends rain on the just and the *unjust alike"* (NLT).

What a mess!

As I exited the makeshift courtroom that usually served as a pastoral office for prayer and counseling, all the commanding ultimatums replayed again and again in my mind. As I walked down the stairs for the last time, his words kept ringing in my ears. "You are banned from our church!" *Banished? Was that actually the word he used?* "Now get out of here and get your office packed and do it now! And make sure you move out of our member's house by the end of today!"

Yes. I had to get all my belongings and get them out of there before the day was over. Packing the office in front of my loving church family and peers was hard. My fellow pastor and friend to this day was in complete shock about my banishment. He was the one who recommended me for the position, and I had assisted him in many areas, including producing the church's first professional, four-color magazine. The reality of what had happened reduced him to heartfelt tears. He had earned the respect of all those who knew or served with him; he had a heart of gold. He was not only upset about having his managing editor removed from his office; he was hurting because he had seen many of the same tactics used on others. This time, however, it was affecting him deeply because he cared for me.

"You are never to come back to this church! Never!" The words kept churning in my mind while I was stuffing my things into every cavity of my van. I knew I had to leave, but where would I go? What would I do? A fellow comrade gave me a few days' pay, but how was that going to get me to who knows where? I was not sure where to go or what to do. Upon turning in my cell phone and keys and hugging my church leaders and friends good-bye, I had one more important call to make before leaving. I had to reach my dear friend Sandy before she walked into this beehive.

Sandy was just a nice young woman I met a few months earlier through a mutual friend. At least this was the story many parishioners were asked to believe. In reality, every time I looked at Sandy Montgomery, I was overwhelmed with symptoms of love—my heart stopped, accompanied by extreme knee wobbling. Professionally, we attempted to be discreet, but how could I keep my powerful feelings of true love under wraps? How was I supposed to behave? After all, we adults holding serious public ministry offices were not allowed to reveal our feelings of complete undying love during Saturday afternoon prayer.

Yet, it was hard to hide my obvious drooling, as I daydreamed about Sandy giving me her hand when I, her valiant knight in shining armor, came galloping up to her on my mighty steed. In a dashing one-arm sweep, I would grasp my "Sunshine Princess," pull her up to my side, and ride out of the church auditorium with everyone standing and staring!

Unfortunately, I had to leave my daydreams behind for the true nightmare I was facing. Was it all a bad dream? I was hoping at any minute to hear my alarm clock buzzing and smell the coffee brewing before I had to leave for the morning prayer time that I enjoyed so much at the church. *This just cannot be happening,* I thought, *since I love these people and we are so close—just like family.* Maybe I had not really been banished at all.

Because of the blur of emotions that whirled through my mind after the brutal confrontation, I did not pause to consider the future. The only thing on my mind was how to accomplish the ultimatum I had been given by nightfall—especially since it was already 4 o'clock in the afternoon when I was tossed out! Wow—banned forever from God's house of prayer! Now, that was a new one for me.

Eventually my mental processes gave way to a preservation layer of near-eternity that escapes capture by the clamor of an immediate moment; you know, the "fantasy-like day-dream" span of seconds in actual time while suspending a seeming period of infinity. Of course, the blink of an eye, or the loud shout of a jealous someone you have temporarily escaped, can jerk you immediately back to the sudden rudeness of earth's reality. Yes, this banishment moment was happening, and I was center stage again—this time in stark contrast to the one in which I had stood that same morning in the chapel's pulpit.

This stage had a trap door where my performance was abruptly ended with the push of a "brother banishment" button. I fell hard, but the landing provided me with a God-ordained entrance ramp onto His highway toward my destiny. It appeared that my dirt road to Heaven was taking a turn, and I was willing to follow as long as I knew it would lead me to the path that God planned. Even though my assignment had gone wacky, I tried to keep my focus on the Kingdom mission.

As a man in the mantle of the prophetic ministry, I was not totally surprised at what happened to me. As a matter of fact, I had been warned in many ways prior to this event in my life. Actually, during the emotional explosion, I had *déjà vu* flashbacks transforming my daydream into reality.

I wondered if this type of outburst is what happens when prophetic people cross the line and enter the world of rules and legalistic orders. Even with prophetic warnings from my spiritual senses, I was not prepared for the dramatic outcome I witnessed in the office that day.

But I knew that experiencing every new step of God's will in my life was the only way to complete the process of becoming a prophet. Surviving those unexpected events of the journey has proven the best instructor for training my spiritual eyes to read God's blueprints. Did this crisis hurt me? Yes—as much as if I had lost a close family member. I realized I would never be able to sit and have fellowship with many dear people I had known. It felt similar to when I had walked into my empty home and realized my family was gone—never to return.

When you are in the moment, it is devastating. Yet even while you are on that low valley road, and groping along in the dark to take the next step, you will be strengthened if you lean upon the arms of your Savior. I did, and He was faithful. All other forms of immediate pain relief for your wounded soul and spirit will take you farther down a road to destruction where there is permanent darkness.

Stunned

Actually driving away from the premises made me understand the reality of what had just taken place. Before your psyche jolts into emergency survival mode, it is as if you awoke in the ditch, immediately following a head-on collision, and you ask yourself, "What just happened to me? I think I was in a serious wreck!" Though I had been accused of far less, the pain and embarrassment I felt might be compared to the shame of a man caught in adultery.

This was not a "megachurch" office where they proclaim to be proponents of God's great family of love for "whosoever." When confronting concerns, they have a "behind-the-scene-approach" of throwing "situations or confrontations" into their quick-remedy *spiritual blender*. As they do, of course, they have all the correct rudiments of the law, including the appropriate "scriptural references" sprinkled over the top—and bye-bye "eye sore."

Other people who were once associated with this church implied that for many years, banishment and hurling problems overboard was common. In fact, there was an ever-growing number of people who were victims of an "unannounced ousting." Over the years I have ministered to the hurts of many of my friends who were former Amish. Never in all my years in the ministry did I think my name would be placed on the pages of statistics that included "banishment" from a modern-day, charismatic, well-known church.

I had been warned; so it was no surprise to go through an inner counsel discussion. These meetings take place frequently in ministry leadership, as in the corporate world, and in all settings that involve people and leadership. We call that working out differences in the backroom behind closed doors. That is normal procedure for handling problems, issues, and situations.

However, when youth and authority and spiritual immaturity are combined, it can produce a religious undercurrent that does not reflect the intentions of the church founders. The situation is similar to backroom politics.

The "Saul Spirit"

I believe that none of it had to happen. With the proper perspective for dealing with circumstances, the leaders and I could have possibly resolved the issue. However, there was no reasoning at that point. As a man who had gone through divorce and "Job style" obliteration, this confrontation did not devastate me, as it did many others who had been treated the same way. When you drive in one evening from a long ministry trip to find an empty home with no family or furnishings, you set up emotional adjusters to handle the next large rock you find in your path. After you have reached your "ground zero" in the journey of your life, you can make it through anything that rolls off the cliff and drops in front of you.

It seems to me that this episode in my life was about more than losing a position at a large church. It was more than God placing me in the framework and trappings of the eyewitness to ministry repositioning. No, this episode involved the spiritual illumination of how our country has evolved in the pursuit of their kings. The "Saul spirit" is still alive, and it is being exposed more and more through an increasing number of fallouts. Humans are the focal point in the ministry. They are the actors in God's plan for advancing *His* Kingdom and not man's.

When a controlling spirit rears its ugly head and takes authority that is beyond God's endorsements, that indicates religious control. When it exercises authority to destroy and not restore lives, that signifies religious control. This is the same spirit that caused the head of John the Baptist to roll, and the one that nailed Jesus to the Cross. This revolting spirit is alive and well today in the religious corridors of the "christianeeze superspiritual"—either you submit to this spirit, or you will be removed. Unless this subversive force is exposed, brought to bear, and dealt with in our "church plants that have yielded to man's ways," we will experience more exoduses from institutionalized forms of worship.

You may need to remember one word of caution as you read through this exposé—love. I do love the pastor and the staff of that very same church from which I was banned. I understand that people are subjected to a variety of (good and evil) forces, and many do not have the solid foundational relationship with the Father through His unconditional love. God had not placed me on an assignment to become the "Righteous Ranger" to single-handedly ride into "religiously infested" churches to marshal suspected violators. No. He simply allowed me to be in certain situations as part of the process of becoming.

God's ultimate creation, humans, are on a life-long pursuit of real love—His love. People in every form of society will continue to adjust from "tyrannical organizations" to alternatives that meet their felt needs. "Felt needs" means they want their needs to be felt and handled compassionately—for real. They want to know that their needs actually count for more than a name on a sign-up sheet to drive a church bus or to bring a dessert to the next church social.

Love Releases the Need to Control

This need to control constituents is one of the reasons why so many people are currently bailing out of the massive church "steamroller" environment, where adherents must live by the unwritten code of conduct—"they bow to our control or they roll!"

I was rolling out of my office and out of the church, for the last time. At this point you are probably thinking that I had committed some serious offense. You have probably been asking yourself just what took place for such a tribunal to have been orchestrated. There was no adulterous affair, no lurking about the church after all the single ladies, there was nothing to merit dismissal. The bottom line: I did not bow down to the controlling spirit. In turn, that allowed the Jezebel influence to create a misguided directive—that they are called to seek and destroy anyone who even appears to have differing views. I was seen as a threat, or even more, a minor challenge to their dogmas. There was no room for "creative thinkers" on this campus! Now it was time for me to leave officially.

God worked out every detail of my journey down yet another unknown path. God began to speak clearly that He had called me to love my enemies and pray for those who persecuted and despitefully used me. My mind did not want to hear Father's voice about that verse. Yet the enemy's voice was right there too, and it was shouting in my mind the reasons for defying orders to vacate the church and not tell anyone about this, not a soul!

The words repeated again and again in my mind like a phone message machine stuck in high volume and repeating the message over and over; this message was quite different from the one delivered on Sunday mornings about love and forgiveness. *"Now get out of here and go get your office packed and do it now! Make sure you also move out of our member's house by the end of today!"*

I looked into the faces of the other pastors who had been brought in as support for the leadership. Only a few hours earlier that day, they had been my ministry family and friends. Now my fellow staff ministers could only display a hopeless blank stare at me with eyes full of hurt and concern—yet positional protection demanded that they remain on the leadership's side of the fence.

The day began quite a bit differently than the afternoon ended. After I had been issued the ultimatum, they covered it with enough technicalities of religious law to ensure they had safety in the assembly of at least three others who were present at the obviously upsetting conference meeting. In the middle of all the blurred lines of demands, from true dedicated ministry to the need for banishment, the purpose and promise of preserving a brother and pastor was definitely not present. How did the action they took lend any help to repair problems on either side of the leadership desk? How did my banishment set an example of the loving Father? Where was Jesus Christ in this picture?

What happened that day was not my idea of a "normal" Christian church setting. But what was normal for me, anyway? I think the only thing normal in my life at that point was the setting on the washing machine. What happened in that meeting was a far cry from any meeting of church leadership I had ever been a part of.

That Day

At the beginning of the day, I was called upon to share a message from the pulpit with the all the pastors and staff at the daily morning devotional meeting. The Lord gave me a specific message that we are to leave a deposit of His blessings wherever we go. And if we never go back to that place again, the people we shared with would have a gift of God's love through His Word that would remain. It proved to be a very timely message ordered by the Holy Spirit.

My Tuesday, July 9, calendar reflected a busy schedule including finalizing the proofs for the first magazine the church was producing; I had much to review and reports to retrieve before a lunch meeting. We had a staff luncheon that very day, which included the senior pastor and the first lady of the church. The church cafe was filled with staff, and the place was a bustle of activity. The size of the church staff was large, because on any given Sunday between 8,000 and 10,000 people attended church services at the various campuses. For comparison, more people attended the morning chapel service, than many churches across our country have in attendance on Sunday morning.

So my day began as the chapel messenger, followed by an important meeting as the managing editor of their premier issue of a major magazine, then to a pastor/prophet luncheon with leadership, and ended with me being thrown out on the street—all before 3 o'clock in the afternoon! The icing on the cake was his command to vacate my living quarters, simply because the owners were long-standing members of the church from which I was now banished.

When I first became a part of the church, it appeared to be the best ministry setting on earth. Encouraged to pray, prophecy, write, minister, etc., I joyfully served God all day and night every single day. The sanctuary looked similar to an enclosed, state-of-the-art sports dome, almost like a convention center. Each day I enjoyed walking through an indoor mall of offices, gymnasiums, media production centers and into my office. I was welcomed and I used my talents to serve God through the church in many capacities. Now it seemed as if I was being crushed for the very process of my mantle. I felt like a rough piece of gravel that an expert Stonemason was shaping, polishing, and preparing to place, at His timing, into a perfectly designed edifice. The process proved its worth by the shape that the Stonemason formed.

The prophetic mantle is from God. It is a gift that gives those who value the King above all others and all motives, abilities to accomplish missions for Him we would otherwise never be able to achieve. The mantle of God for your calling is precious.

I was given a prophetic word a number of years prior to the "banishment" meeting at the church. The prophet said, "The Lord has designed a very powerful prophetic mantle for you. However, the mantle that was designed to crush the enemy, if not cared for through the proper instructions and obedience to God, then that which was designed to crush the enemy will instead crush the man!" I thank God that He gave me the strength to endure; though my heart felt crushed, the crushing supplied me with more than enough of Jesus' blood to continue to flow in the anointing of God.

That documented and accurate prophecy has always stayed with me in my spirit. I have great reverence for God's mantle of anointing. When God spoke, I wanted to hear only His voice and obey. About three months before the "banishment" meeting, I had been told by at least three credible prophetic voices that I would be in a meeting and would be released from my present assignments! You may wonder why I would go through the pain and suffering if I had been forewarned. I say that prophetic fulfillment is like being told that a tornado may hit your house in about three hours. You are a believer in devout prayer to God, and you are rebuking the wind and believing to turn the tide of the storm. You are still a resident of that location. Three hours pass, and sure enough, here comes the tornado. Only it is not a category 2, it is an F5 storm—a severe one. You are in the back room of your home praying, faith hits you, and you go to the front porch and point your finger at the blackened sky with a funnel cloud headed toward you. You scream, "In the Name of Jesus, I decree we will live and not die!"

About that time the tornado tears your house to pieces! Miraculously, all of you survive. Did God keep His word? Absolutely. Meanwhile, next door at the park, people had crowded under the dugout with about a hundred children. They had stopped their cussing and were following the lead of the God-fearing saints to "command the storm over and away from them and to protect each child!" God arranged to answer both prayers.

You have insurance on your home and your family is OK. No life was lost and we can construct new buildings. To make it better, old Tom the drunk, little Tommy's grandpa, found Jesus in the middle of a baseball field in the midst of the storm. So many times that is how the prophetic prayer and declaration works; yet people fail to realize the multiple aspects of answered prayers.

Storms and Battles

I saw the storm brewing, and God sent a local prophet to me a couple of weeks before the meeting. Also, a precious "spiritual mom" of mine called me to ask how I was doing—the day before the meeting! She consulted with me over a word from God about her specific need and then did something she had never done before. She said God had given her a word for me! I was interested to hear what she had to say, especially since I knew her well and respected her international ministry, as did many others.

"I want to tell you what I saw in my prayer time with the Lord," she said. She went on to say that she saw me in a vision-type dream, and I was going into a tribunal of some sort. She continued, "It was like a battlefront meeting, and the officers were first meeting with you, but then started firing bullets at you. You had a resolve as a face of 'flint,' and the bullets flew all around you, but not one hit you. They were upset because you would not change your mind-set to match theirs!"

Wow! She told me that she felt the Lord wanted me to "set your face like flint and do not defend nor retaliate, simply stay the ground and do not give in to this demand. Set your face like flint and God will bring you on through to the other side." Yes, God did get me through to the other side! Nonetheless, I got shoved around a bit in the process of moving from the back room to the front porch to command the storm not to destroy me. When you are the one who has received the prophesy about getting through the storm, you'll have ample warning to prepare yourself spiritually.

I was certainly "fasted and prayed up," as I had just ended the longest fast of my life. Furthermore, because of my ministry post, and as a single pastor, I had a schedule that seemed to involve fasting, praying, and ministering 24/7. I had received a word of knowledge and wisdom from the Lord through my spiritual mom and other prophetic voices. When it played out, I was not simply "speechless in my spirit," because a storm is still a storm! I have phrased this many times while teaching in our prophetic schools, "*Knowing* it is still not going through it."

Sometimes you have done all the fasting, praying, and decreeing you can do, and the storm keeps coming straight at you! That means it is time to square your shoulders, set your face like flint, and lean straight into the storm's approach. You are then doing what I term the "above all, stand" part of Ephesians 6:13: *"Therefore, take up the full armor of God, that you will be able to resist in the evil day, and having done everything, to stand firm"* (NASB).

This Scripture is one of my favorites, because it is not a defensive posture! In their day it was an offensive position of that part of their battle. This posture means using God's wisdom not to give up in the middle of the raging storm. Soldiers during that time would stand beside each other and lock their large shields together, forming a protective covering from the enemy's arrows and fiery darts. The shields even contained a certain substance that would extinguish the flames. As the soldiers held their ground without fighting back, the enemy advanced toward them.

When they were close enough, the soldiers drew out their swords and, in formation with shields still locked together, they became a large, unified enemy destroyer.

The focus when you are in the battle is not for others to say, "Well, he took it like a brave person should!" The focus should be to win the battle and complete the assignment God gave you by joining forces, and uniting with others in fasting and prayer. We must use our wits in the middle of the storm or battle. If I alone jumped out into the battlefield while all my comrades were locking their shields and standing, I would become quick pickings for the enemy! Sadly, there may be times when you are hit with "friendly fire" if you are out of position. The captain may say "Charge," and the spears are released—and you are 20 steps ahead! Being out of position can be painful and even deadly. Remember, above all—stand until you hear God telling you to move forward.

Where does real love fit in the middle of a storm or battle? Love never demands its own way. The Master Creator allows us to experience the trouble, but He has made a way for us to survive. He shapes the stone for His purpose—and the process of becoming a precious gem depends on our reliance on and faith in Him. Regardless what the church leaders said that day, the decision was ultimately up to the Lord. Love offers itself up to the Master Creator to decide whether or not this stone is the "keystone" or one that needs to be crushed for roadway gravel.

Jesus was crushed for us—the Master knows the eternal purpose of the stone. We simply need to be in love with the Creator. As that love and trust is conveyed to Him, the same Creator shares His agape love with us. As the One Who created Heaven and earth in its entire splendor, He can easily rearrange gravel to create a precious gem.

Since that "day of banishment" I have reflected upon those events and have set out on a quest to grow deeper in my relationship with the Father. During this journey I have crossed paths with Don Nori, friend and founder of Destiny Image Publishers, who introduced me to a collection of appointed language in the Father's pen of love. I believe you will enjoy reading Don's book, *Romancing the Divine*.

THE PERIL OF TRUE LOVE

Love without legalism; commitment without control; fullness without fear; relationship without religion—the very mention of such possibilities brings feelings of exhilaration and hope, for these are the deepest yearnings of our souls, the essence of true love.

Unfortunately, these passions of the heart are foreign to many of today's teachings, that to harbor such intimate thoughts may border on heresy. That is the peril of true love. It is the inevitable price of longing. But when one has fallen hopelessly, desperately, and eternally in love, nothing is predictable, and nothing is ordinary. In fact, it turns the average person into a hopelessly lovesick and desperate human being. Love transforms the way he thinks, the things he does, and the way he prays. True love changes his view of life and determines his reason for living.

In Don Nori's descriptive opening in "The Perils of True Love" chapter of *Romancing the Divine*, he unveils the secrets to satisfying your hunger for God. As you discover these secrets, your relationship with the Father will deepen as never before.

"The invasion of true love into the heart of any human being turns that person into someone quite extraordinary indeed. For nothing...*nothing* will ever be the same again. Nothing else will satisfy as it once satisfied, nothing else will ever be worth living for." Nori confirms through revelation that "Love will cause one to take risks that make a normal person shudder...."

Many "church people" are fed up with all the man-made institutionalized food handed to them by good-intentioned but loveless leaders. These people are searching for God-made food with true love as the main ingredient that reveals their reason for living. Give us more real love. We want the true love of the Father.

Nori writes:

...love makes God real.

True love destroys the way religion has told us faith is supposed to be. Love ignores her critics and yields to the sweet comfort of desire deep within the human heart.

True love never ends and can never be destroyed. True love cannot be reasoned with, nor can it be reasoned away, for it has little to do with the intellect but it has everything to do with that which the intellect can never touch. True love dwells so much higher than understanding, in a dimension where love rules and the mind serves true love.

Love will always, always, find a way.

If she is ridiculed, it is an understandable, acceptable price. True love will never sing the songs of a hollow religion and is not pacified with pointless ritual. Love cannot coexist with legalism and does not interact well with hypocrisy.

If she is banished, it is a good thing, for it will allow more time to be with the Lord. If she is condemned, she will smile quietly, respectably, of course.

Condemnation is the last course of a clueless man.

Love cannot be condemned.

Love always prevails.

Love always gathers.

Love always forgives.

Love always heals.

Love understands.

Love feeds the world with compassion and mercy.

True love yields to the forgiving nature of her Lord and accurately represents His grace in every respect.

Love lives forever.

As for the stale complexities of religion, they will change. Someone possessing more courage than fear will face off with the ghosts of yesterday and the dusty echoes they represent, returning God's people to the simplicity and the joy of loving God.[1]

THE LOVE CHAPTER

Well and rightfully known as "the love chapter," First Corinthians chapter 13 is worth reading more than once. As you ponder God's love, reflect on the previous selections taken from the book, *Romancing the Divine*. Please read and meditate upon His Word in a relaxed pace and in a comfortable setting.

If I speak with the tongues of men and of angels, but do not have love, I have become a noisy gong or a clanging cymbal. And if I have the gift of prophecy, and know all mysteries and all knowledge; and if I have all faith, so as to remove mountains, but do not have love, I am nothing. And if I give all my possessions to feed the poor, and if I surrender my body to be burned, but do not have love, it profits me nothing. Love is patient, love is kind, and is not jealous; love does not brag and is not arrogant, does not act unbecomingly; it does not seek its own, is not provoked, does not take into account a wrong suffered, does not rejoice in unrighteousness, but rejoices with the truth; bears all things, believes all things, hopes all things, endures all things.

Love never fails; but if there are gifts of prophecy, they will be done away; if there are tongues, they will cease; if there is knowledge, it will be done away. For we know in part, and we prophesy in part; but when the perfect comes, the partial will be done away. When I was a child, I used to speak as a child, think as a child, reason as a child; when I became a man; I did away with childish things. For now we see in a mirror dimly, but then face to face; now I know in part, but then I shall know fully just as I also have been fully known. But now faith, hope, love, abide these three; but the greatest of these is love (1 Corinthians 13:1-13 NASB).

ALL YOU NEED IS *True* LOVE

During my unusual sojourn on the prophetic path, people asked me how I could talk and write about love so much. The truth is that I would not be able to understand God's voice to hear in the prophetic mode without knowing God's love. A person has to know God to be able to love. If we know God, we will know love. God is love.

A real love story with a happy ending is all I ever really wanted—what we all want. Most people tell me that they want a genuine love with their best friend, who is a partner in their calling from God. This, and the best romance drama all wrapped up in one special package from Heaven with our names on it, is what we truly want from this sojourn. We want to be loved and to love—we have a desire to love built into our hearts. At one time or another during life, most people have felt cheated of this gift of love from Heaven; yet in the back of their minds, they know there exists a secluded dream demanding a life with a fantasy-like ending.

When I tell people this, it becomes a living testimony to the ladies and men who thought that, because they had jumped too quickly in the past, genuine love had passed them by forever. Maybe you are one who doesn't hope anymore—who will not even consider the possibility of finding a happily-ever-after love. Well, get ready to dream again, because failure is not your fate! God did not create you to fail—He is the restorer of your soul. He gives life and gives it more abundantly. Get ready to be transformed by a present day, real-life love story that proves God is a keeper of His promises!

Life seemed to be pulling love out of my grip, no matter how hard I tried to embrace it. Have you ever felt that you were grabbing at romance, but it was too elusive? Then let me tell you, I can provide the hope you need. Throughout the years, the dreams I held within my heart dared to materialize a few times, only to have them dashed upon the rocks—draining the life out of the dreams of my very soul. Each time, it felt as if my emotions were being dragged into the gutter. Then I learned how to absorb this divine destiny builder for my life. You can too. Realize that everything works together for good for those who love the Lord (see Rom. 8:28).

I am living proof that all the things that happened in my life were leading up to the time when I found my true love here on earth. This last chance almost eluded me, but God's providence and many prayers provided healing, love, acceptance, forgiveness, and many miracles that allowed my life drama to unfold with amazing results!

Yes, prayers are answered. Yes, God does want you to experience the love of your life! Did Jesus tell the woman at the well in Samaria to run quickly ahead of him to make everything perfect so they could hold a city hall discussion about ways to form a more perfect Samaria? No! In spite of all her past failures, Jesus loved the woman into her destiny! He is trying to do that for all of us—but we have to allow Him to do so. Forget the past and look forward to your future, knowing that God has your best as His interest. He created you in His image and knows your every thought and dream. He can and will help you. I decree that you will see your vision come true.

Does the story of Cinderella still stir within your heart the desire for your very own fairy-tale romance or true love from God? Do you really enjoy watching romance movies like *Sleepless in Seattle, Ghost, or An Affair to Remember*? How can you not believe that God will lift you higher than any of the demons of defeat? You know He not only can, but will. Settle into a comfortable chair and turn off your TV, because God has a future for you that will go beyond any man-made movie or show.

Let your dreams soar again as your spirit reaches new heights. Allow your hopes to ascend beyond your routine daily existence. Allow your dream chords to be fine-tuned—at last—into harmony with the divine promises He has destined you to claim.

He knows what and whom you need to accomplish your calling and destiny. Your real-life drama will reveal more than a few "happy endings" along the way—expect them, welcome them no matter how big or small. Do not allow the enemy to rob you of the joy of dreaming your dreams!

PROCEED—WITH CAUTION

As you inhale fresh revelation from God, step with boldness away from the destroyers of dreams. The enemy lurks around your visions and, at your faintest whisper of hope to find true love, he tries to pounce in and destroy your dream. The enemy comes in many different forms, including: religious piety, warped theology, and unrighteous "concern."

Following God's path often means breaking "man's rules" that were formed from a mixture of societal codes and a plethora of religious rhetoric. Choosing to follow God's path sounds easy; but the process is hard, because man's route is usually gift wrapped and hand-delivered as concern—despite its appealing look, it usually dislocates your future. Successfully following God's path requires that you become a warrior who is serious about defending your hopes and dreams. As you yield yourself to God's will, your obedience will please the King of kings—and the Kingdom will be yours on earth as it is in Heaven.

Please discover this one thing through this chronicle of candor: you are more than able to find and live your dream. As you enter the realm of revived hope, I pray you will be encouraged while learning from my mistakes. I hope yours will be a smoother journey with very few detours. God prepares the path for each of us with great care; and each of His vessels is unique in the hands of the Master Craftsman. The result of filling pages with a panorama of intense demonstrations to make your dreams seem more valuable to the mission, would only serve to tarnish the instrument. Furthermore, we must learn as crushed stone presented by Jesus' providence to pave the road to reach the next destination.

Rest assured this small journal of mine is primarily developed as a scroll for the King's court in which He has approved my spirit to now deliver His hope to the nations. In that vein, those whom God directs to acquire proof by a record of unseasonably long periods in the desert regions have a tenacity to find their promised land of love and will not be disappointed. For those with courageous hearts who dare to become chasers of the real dreams that come true, you must realize that you will receive the parchment containing His map and compass. You will also be invited into His very courts and will leave with the keys of life.

This account of my life provides reality in your own quest. I have found that many people depend only on the hope of a high-speed file retrieval system to supply a cosmetic rescue mechanism that "might" help solve a dilemma. Unfortunately, many pursue the Kingdom of Love from an outward approach—disregarding the issues of their hearts—and thus are constantly feeding a growing monster of desire which is controlled by their lifestyles. This causes a meandering about in the outer courts, driven by the carnal demands of feeding the insatiable appetites of their flesh.

Depending on and trusting God's love for me is the only way to completely solve all of life's dilemmas. Only He can set things right that seem totally out of control. Only His path leads to deep down resolution and eternal peace.

I believe that my life and ministry's purpose in the Kingdom of God is to represent Jesus Christ and His precept to love one another. The only one I need to please is Him. As my relationship with the Father deepens, it becomes more apparent to me that many of us have been following a counterfeit path filled with a "busyness" that enslaves us and causes us to focus on things other than our journey's purpose.

Release your hearts to His and come with a reckless abandon for His genuine love. How much will it cost for this journey? Simply everything! Be prepared to pay the price of family, friends, associations, plans, perspective, and your will. However, the price you will pay pales in comparison to the glory which will be revealed to you through His love. Believe me, every price we pay and every sacrifice we make is worth it.

Love Never Fails

By using the pen and placing my life on paper, I am demonstrating before the world that no matter my predicaments—the good, the bad, and the downright dirty—there is always hope! God takes the ones who are willing to go through the fires and have all the binders burned off their lives, and provides them freedom from their religious captors. He knows that we for too long have been shaped by the ignorance of unfounded teachings. I present this book as a God-ordained message for the edification of God's people—to provide hope and healing for the hopeless. I know that no matter how low we feel and whatever devastation is allowed to enter our lives, we can still be anointed and powerfully used by God to give Him glory!

I do not seek the approval of the world or man for my life's content. Seeking an approval rating by today's "established church order" would have caused me to conceal the genuine, personal account of my life's experiences as evidence—and hope. In the face of our religious banishment, I believe it is important to expose real-life trials, troubles, and things no one wants to admit, even the things that provoke hearts to question years of theological foundations. Then we can become God's living voice, entreating us to genuinely answer the question, "What are you going to do with a love like that?"

Although those who have helped create my life examples may not publicly agree that the entire story needs to be told, most of them will respect the purpose. Over the years the leadership in many churches has allowed the teaching of questionable doctrine, supporting man's pride and extinguishing his desire for the "unadulterated Truth of God." Too often we allow "spiritual cataracts" to blur our heart's vision of God's Kingdom, and we become blinded to His presence as well. But God knows how to grab the leaders' attention. He allows their statistics to fall, the very numbers that have become the goal to gauge spiritual success—unfounded and inflated figures that lead to spiritual market crashes.

The truth, God's truth, is the only way to keep from being crushed along the journey. Religion must have a scapegoat. Jesus was the perfect sacrifice who offered pure conviction of sin. Let His sacrifice be enough! We can allow the Lord, through His great mercy and love, to begin to deal with our own situations, or simply choose to refuse His help. Remember, waiting to ask God for help until "later" will make matters worse—as evidenced by my life of ups and downs. Procrastination then, if it lasts long enough, leaves God with no choice but to allow massive spiritual earthquakes to realign hearts to conform to His Kingdom and His plans.

Nevertheless, bear in mind that you will not wander alone into this melodrama of ink-filled pages, with allowances for fear of your sinister foe. You will slam the gates of doubt closed before the dream crusher can destroy hope's invitation again. You will go past the courts of the mundane and enter the lush land of vibrant visions, with God's pledge that your new dream is dawning. Your horizons of hope will allow dreams to be realized for the reality of God's best for you. This is about love that is irrevocably the seasoning that will come through your hunger and patience for more.

Too many times we have longed for more, only to discover another closed door. Too often our lives have been as shattered as our dreams, but there was hope in Christ and He delivered the keys to unlock the doors you find along your path to becoming. The journey is not to achieve man's idea of success day by day. Rather it is to find the heart of the Father and His plans for His Kingdom. Doubters and dream-busters have mishandled destiny's doorknobs long enough. The Father's longing look into your life will be answered with your confident "Yes"—this time you will have a starring role in the *True Love Story from Heaven!*

Only through our trials and tears, dilemmas and defeat, can we learn how to use these situations as fuel to ignite the fire of hope. Those fires warm our hearts as they yearn for the truth that now accelerates a demand with desperation that leads us to victory no man or beast of religion can restrain. Our journey will one day become an invaluable *journal* demonstrating what God has done for others, through us! My journal is filled with miracles—yours will be, too.

Your hopes and dreams will take on new meanings, as A *True Love Story from Heaven* changes your life! After you begin the journey of genuine love, the kind that offers both acceptance and forgiveness, you will do anything to stay on the path. Our Father has made us an eternal promise through giving us His only Son to take our place in redeeming us sinners from the sins of the world so that we can know true love.

Chasing after this love all my life, I finally came to understand the way to obtain it. I had to submit to and accept God's will as the Savior displayed with His death to reconcile Himself and His family together forever! The greatest test a lasting love relationship can face is the death of our desire for the very one we love. We must "die to self," which enables us to receive a relationship that considers someone else's worth more important than our own.

Will we make it through this journey? Can real love ever be obtained while living here on this earth? Dare to travel down the path of the overly desperate who believe dying is the only way to discover eternal love. The unconditional love you pursue is achievable. The love you hunger for is within your reach. Unconditional love, a loving relationship, and your dreams are all possible. Please do not give up—you are closer than you think to achieving your destiny! God has made enough provisions for you, and my prayer is that you discover His provision as you continue on your mission. The mission is the process and it is that process that tailors the mantle. In the end, the process provides the fit.

Along our journey's search, we must exhaust all our efforts to find *Him*—not a plan. This is the message of His true love story from Heaven! The plan is in *His* hand.

Endnote

1. Don Nori. *Romancing the Divine* (Shippensburg, PA: Destiny Image Publishers, 2006), 8-10.

CHAPTER 7

Unconditional Love Means Unconditional Forgiveness

GOD'S LOVE IS UNCONDITIONAL—NO MATTER WHAT

God is all about unconditional love. Unconditional? Without a clause? No strings attached? No conditions? Yes, that is God's love.

All who have had the privilege of being raised in any form of evangelical Christian church over the past few decades have heard First Corinthians, chapter 13, or the "love chapter" in the New Testament.

It is not rude, it is not self-seeking, it is not easily angered, and it keeps no record of wrongs (1 Corinthians 13:5 NIV).

"Keeps no record of wrongs" is one phrase that certainly ties in with the idea of unconditional love and unconditional forgiveness; however, something has happened to the *practice* of the one gift God deemed as *"the greatest of these...."*

OK, so perhaps you are thinking, "Here comes the Louisville Slugger sermon coated with the *love* commandment, because no one helped at the homeless shelter last week!" Relax. That is not my style.

Fairness has never been the question in understanding the love our Father has for us. He loves us unconditionally, and that is not an easy concept to understand or to accept. The reason: we exist in an environment that accepts that we behave in response to how we have been treated. In other words, you do me right, and I will return the favor. You take me to lunch and next week I'll take you to lunch. We pretend not to live by that unwritten rule, but when our kindnesses are not returned as expected, we will usually terminate that relationship.

As hard as it is to love those who do not reciprocate our kindnesses or show compassion to us when life is throwing us troubles, we who follow our Savior have no recourse but to repay others with the love of Jesus. We have no excuse for continuing the pattern of "lovelessness" displayed in many of today's religious institutions. God's pattern for all is true love. The true love of the Father offers acceptance and forgiveness—no matter what! "No matter what" causes religious spirits to become unnerved! Have you ever wondered why? It is because the *"no matter what"* kind of love demands no form of control. That kind of love requires our total surrender to the Father's control. This causes "control freaks" to become very angry, as I found out on "banishment day" when I did not retaliate.

Some people play mind games so complex that when a person being attacked does not retaliate, it actually makes them drop their guard, weakening their defense mechanism, and making them vulnerable. There are too many mental chess games being played today, when all that is needed is the genuine love of the Lord exemplified to us through His only begotten Son, Jesus Christ.

LET GOD CONTROL

We have to stop worrying about "repressed guilt feelings" that satan resurrects from our religious-based training and continues to use to attack our consciences. Lighten up. Your daughter's recital *is* the most important thing. Listening to your spouse's concern *is* the most important thing. Ministry is love of our family—God's primary church model. For Jesus Christ, His physical family was somewhat integrated with His ministry family. Regardless of whether I am in a remote region of Tibet or in the center of some charismatic, megachurch stadium, the Kingdom of God is the goal.

Next, enter the enemy who does not play fair—ever! The enemy infiltrates churches in the form of a religious spirit of control and is usually cloaked in a designer suit of austere righteousness. More than one person has been tossed aside as the enemy validates questions in leaders' minds of seeming rebelliousness as witchcraft that could lead their entire flock of thousands straight into hell. When so convicted, they justify the slaughter of one for the perceived safety and love of the whole. I do not believe that was what the Lord was referring to when Jesus taught the parable about the one lost sheep and leaving the 99 to find it. A self-righteous religious spirit destroys from within and causes serious damage.

BACK TO "THE DAY"

Driving off the parking lot with the huge church behind me, I felt as devastated as if being burned at the stake or hung from a tree while everyone watched.

I had no place to go—no family in the region. My mother had died less than two months before, and yet I had served God, this church, and the leadership with all I had in my spirit to give. It had been less than two years earlier when I arrived home to find an empty house—no wife, no children, no furnishings. To say that the trauma to my moral fiber was severe from absorbing the emotional barrage inflicted by divorce and the death of my dear mother would be an understatement.

Most people who have faced multiple traumas, which I learned during one of my godly counselor sessions tailored for wounded ministers, may be institutionalized, have turned to drinking or drugs, committed suicide, or at best, evaporated from society. I did think about all those options, but God came to me through the prayers of loving people who helped place His loving arms around me. It was not an easy transition from church staff member to the unknown. Yet, His love intercepted my broken spirit and set me back on the path to becoming His servant.

Yes, this was the time to take my next step in the journey, the kind that never really ends until you stand before the Father in Heaven. From faith-filled praying, preaching, and prophesying all day and night, I was banished and sent suddenly to destiny's door!

I called Sandy to tell her what happened. Miraculously, she answered the phone. I caught her just seconds before she was going out the door to attend a monthly ladies' meeting at the same church from which I was driving away from for the last time. God's perfect timing allowed us to connect before she left for the meeting. What a caring God!

My voice was shaking uncontrollably as I called, and she asked why my voice seemed so different. She also asked why I was calling, since we had agreed not to phone, write, or even speak to each other for the next five to seven years, and then we were to be married. It seemed like an eternity to wait but we knew God Himself had put us together forever! We had agreed to this difficult delay in our destiny because we were both in a position of complete and total submission to the will of God for our lives.

Since I was submitted to God, I was also under the authority of my pastor and spiritual covering. He had instructed that I wait this length of time to be married, in order to travel the world and minister with him to the nations.

I had no idea how to tell Sandy that I had been banished from the church because of her. I did not know how to say that she was the "labeled reason" I was thrown out of the church, my job, and my residence. Knowing the matter must have been important enough to break the five-to-seven year distance agreement, Sandy allowed me to come see her and tell her face to face the events that transpired.

Still in a state of utter shock, I arrived at Sandy's door. She had on a beautiful red suit for an early meeting with one of the leaders at the church. She took one look at me and wondered what happened. I explained as best I could.

Please Release Me and Let Me Love

"Sandy, I'm so sorry. Please understand that I never wanted any of this to happen, and I don't want you to be hurt. If you go to your women's meeting, you may face a new and terribly uncomfortable situation." When I told her I had been released today from my pastoral position, she immediately responded, "Praise God forever! Praise Jesus! He answers fervent prayers quickly! Thank You, Jesus! Thank you, Jesus! Thank You Holy Spirit!" She recounted for me how she, much like Hannah in the

Bible, had travailed in fervent passionate prayer before Almighty God *all night long*—the night before "banishment day."

Sandy told me not to worry because God will have His way, and that everything was going to be just fine. Then she asked me to wait outside for a few minutes. She went inside and reappeared wearing blue jeans and a pullover shirt. She said we needed to take my van and retrieve all my personal belongings from my temporary living quarters as requested by the church leader.

Oh what a charge her enthusiastic and positive attitude was to my almost completely fried battery of emotions. Having a true friend and someone I loved so deeply reach out and care meant more to my survival that day than anything anyone else could have done. She did not judge me on the outward appearance of what happened. She discerned what the Father was saying through the situation, and through that understanding knew how to help.

We made the time count and accomplished the difficult assignment of removing my personal items from the home of the dear couple who loved me. I had lived with them for over one year, and we had become family. This precious saint told me, "God has that perfect lady for you so just stay right here and wait on Him." Sandy and I were careful not to mention the details of what had happened at the church that day. Even though the move was abrupt, they were loving, understanding, and quiet during my exodus. I chose to say only loving and positive comments, and Sandy quoted encouraging Scriptures while she lovingly helped pack. The Holy Spirit was creating an atmosphere of true love in the middle of devastation. I knew that anything else said to explain the situation would give the enemy more fuel and possibly cause a major delay in the healing process for all parties involved.

ONE MOVE LEADS TO ANOTHER

After all my personal items were loaded into my van, I drove back to Sandy's house, parked, and took my first "Selah." What in the name of serving Almighty God's purpose, had happened that day? I had gone from delivering the morning devotions at church, to being banished from God's House of Prayer, to sitting on Sandy's patio furniture drinking a glass of cool water. Now here I was sitting in a lawn chair talking to the most beautiful woman, inside and out, that I had ever known. What in the great scheme of life did God want me to do next?!

I thanked Sandy very much for offering to allow me to stay in her garage apartment, under the mutual agreement that our relationship remain completely honorable before God—as it had always been. She called a friend to stay with her 24/7 as a "chaperone" to help us avoid even the appearance of evil. Although we were attracted to each other, because I was in a Christian leadership position, we knew not to do anything that would destroy our destiny. Now, during the aftermath of the day's battle, Sandy was the most caring and compassionate person I had ever met. She was a real "friend in need" sort of a person who helped me regain my senses. Just knowing that I had a place to lay my head that night gave me peace. I felt as if I had just returned from the front lines of a major firefight and had landed in a city of refuge. This was the healing balm from Heaven to my ravaged soul.

This new beginning of my sojourn advanced my walk from the desert to the valley. We then obeyed the Father further, and this process has consistently led us up from the valley toward the top of the Mountain of God! This journey is not about arriving, rather it is about the process on the pathway to God. Jesus Christ partook of the Father's request to offer us more enriched orders than filling a pew in some building we call a church. Knowing and loving God is all about surrendering to His order—not ours, or our "doing church" the way others think it should be done. It doesn't matter where or when you meet to worship Him.

After you find this freedom that is associated with love, acceptance, and forgiveness, you can then follow the process that has been assigned for your life in the journey for dominion in the Kingdom of God on earth as it is in Heaven! It is here; it is for you; and it is available for you now—and forever!

Go with me for a while down this road to ponder some thoughts you may have had about others you have met. Do you remember meeting a stranger who did not talk much, did not attract lots of attention toward himself, yet you seemed drawn to that person? I have. This type of person listens to your every word and smiles convincingly at your need for approval and understanding. This person quietly slips out unnoticeably to pick up a dropped notebook or collect coffee cups around a meeting table while others visit or talk. It is not a performance, as this person's actions are simply a way of life.

They are the ones we go to for that quiet solitude of caring conversation because we feel unconditional acceptance in their presence. Jesus modeled this for us with His ministry infusion of love to His intimate ministry family—His disciples and close family members. Jesus fed thousands with a miraculous meal from a lad's basket, and He consistently continues to hand out manna—bread of Heaven—to those with hearts desperate for words of life and freedom in serving the King as residents of His Kingdom.

Unconditional love defines Sandy's countenance. To enjoy the total feeling of unconditional acceptance in her presence makes me want to be like that deep within my spirit. I could not help but love her as I had fallen in love with her on the phone even before we met in person. Since the Lord God spoke to Sandy and told her not to meet me in person for two weeks after we first spoke on the phone, we did not allow "flesh" to enter our relationship. I fell in love with her—a completely sold out and on fire for Jesus, godly lady. After many long and wonderful conversations, I knew God planned for me to marry Sandy. I agreed with Him and therefore I set out on a relentless pursuit of making her feel the same way. Time and time again I lavished her with 12 beautiful red roses, countless love letters, and numerous gifts. She was the "one" God had promised through a prophet who would be my seven times greater ministry partner and I was sure of it.

No Strings Attached

When I awoke the next morning, I felt extreme solace. As I began to focus on my new surroundings and reality slowly drifted in, the realization that what had happened was not a dream slowly permeated into my spirit. Waking up in a safe place was like being washed ashore on a beautiful island after being tossed from a ship.

I thanked Sandy again for providing shelter for me as we sat near the huge Southern Pecan tree in her backyard and discussed the past, present, and future. During the throes of "banishment day," I had thoughts that my future whereabouts might include some no-name town in Mexico; sitting here with Sandy was much the opposite! I had no desire to ever leave her, but how could I ask her to marry me again now with no job, home, and no way to provide for her? All these thoughts were racing through my mind at once.

I felt as if the spiritual battles I had experienced were manned with hell's special forces, and I had confronted battalions of religious spirits head on. I was not supposed to survive. Now here I was having a "normal" conversation with a woman who cared about me. Sandy said that God had told her she would be restored in marriage to her "Mr. Right" in her near future. And now here we were, discussing the future under that same pecan tree where God had spoken to her just before we met.

We discussed the words God had given to each of us. This was not our first marriage and we were not 20-something going into this relationship with "blind desire." When I arrived on her doorstep the day that I left the church, I had planned to warn her, and to tell her that I did not want my troubles to involve or hurt her in any way. Now, we were discussing a life together and the prospect of completing my assignment and my calling for God. My calling from God was the most important thing to Sandy.

As we talked, I recalled every detail of the prophetic words that had recently been given over me by a prophet in a large church in Atlanta, Georgia. I had been assigned to take a group of pastors who were visiting from an Atlanta church for a "look-see" tour of our church. During dinner one evening, one of the men said, "Prophet, I have a word for you!"

I replied kindly, yet meaningfully, "Who will cover your word that it is from the Lord?" One of the other pastors at the table immediately piped in, "Man of God, this is our house prophet and you had been in Atlanta and had given a word over him, the bishop, and the leaders there. We cover his word as pastors!"

"OK, give me the now word," I said. Oh, did he ever!

I received the following supportive and accurate word. "Prophet John Mark Pool, you will soon meet your 'seven-times-greater-than-ever' ministry partner and wife-of-your-life. You will also know this by the fact that despite all your battles and wars, you are about to come into a time with God that will bring you up and out of your desert. You will know this because as you have given up houses, land, ministries, and family, know that I, the Lord, am giving all that back to you as well. You will have land you did not buy, wells you did not dig, houses you did not build, and a ministry that will touch the nations with My prophetic word through you. You are coming into your season of shifting into your restoration. Soon, My son, it will be very soon. This is not months from now, it is soon you will meet this lady."

When they picked me up from the restaurant floor, I asked him how much he actually knew about me. He said very little, as he had known me only the short time we had been together at his church in Atlanta. I was overwhelmed! At the time, I was still living with my precious spiritual family and momma at my "prophet's quarters." By then my life had been reduced to a ministry van and a 30- by 20-foot storage building full of the various items left in my life. Now a prophet was telling me my future was going to be blossoming roses! It just came out—the famous "Sarah laugh." (What Abraham's wife did when she heard she was going to conceive Isaac!) I began to ask forgiveness but said to him, "Sir, with all due respect for your efforts as a prophetic voice, might I inform you of my condition in life? I am living in a bedroom in an older section of town with my spiritual parents and all my life is oozing out behind me, leaving a trail of tears and destruction that no one else would ever want to follow. So, be advised that although this sounds almost impossible to receive, it is way out there!"

This was a man who was accustomed to hearing from God and did not flinch at my response, except to add more fuel to the fire. "Oh, so you want to laugh like Sarah and not have a thought of faith to accept this word? Then hear the Word of the Lord that says, 'You have two daughters who do not live in this state, and they will be coming to stay with you soon; and your seven-times-greater-than wife and ministry partner who is about to be in your life will be a friend, even as another mother in their lives! The oldest daughter is much more like your personality and carries your same prophetic mantle of anointing in her life!"

There was no more laughter. God grabbed my attention. The prophetic voice operating under such an anointing can grab the attention suddenly, too! When the Lord allows an "unknown voice" in your life that is accountable to both proper spiritual authority and God to "read your mail," (especially that which no one has ever opened before), God should always receive your undivided attention. He sure did receive mine!

Now I was seriously sober. This man from Atlanta could not have known that specific information except from God. Even if he knew I had two daughters living back in Texas with their mother and new stepfather, I realized only God and I knew the details he supplied. This was very interesting now—to say the least! The Atlanta prophet added, "You will also meet this woman within three days!"

As I have learned many things while sojourning in this bizarre mantle known as the prophetic, one thing the good Lord has taught me—only give specific times and dates if the Lord audibly tells you! Even then, I almost always want to have God tell me more than once, if possible! Either my faith or my past made me understand that is about the fastest way to become a "non-credible" voice—giving specifics and then having nothing happen. When a prophet releases a specific date and time, it has to happen during that time frame, or the prophecy is about 99 percent of the time not of God. It is important to understand that time in prophetic language involves variables and conditions that always exist.

The following is a small sidebar for those interested in more schools of thought about the prophetic calling. When I received additional prophetic training, what I just mentioned about language and variables was confirmed and taught by another seasoned prophet. Prophet Mike told me that if I wanted the devil to destroy my prophetic future, the fastest way possible would be for me to decree a time and date to a prophetic word when God did not reveal it to me.

The Atlanta group left for home, and I was back in the office on Monday morning at the church. I was visiting with my immediate manager and pastor over the media and network ministry while standing in our office parking lot. A mutual friend, Brother Ronnie Karidolf, who is a Holy Ghost prayer warrior, a highly respected and loved pastor, and is extremely gifted in the prophetic gifts of God, came over to talk to me.

"Pastor Mark, do you mind if I give the wild prophet's business card to a beautiful young woman who needs a real godly friend right now?" I reached into my pocket and gave him my ministry business card to give to Sandy Montgomery. As I handed him the card I said, "Well, I am for sure not interested in a wife because of all I have been through the past few years, but a friend to talk to sounds nice. Just mention my name and give her my card and have her call me and e-mail me at this address."

Sure enough, my friend took off—he says he had never played "cupid" before—to relay the information. Soon my friend reappeared and said, "Ahem, excuse me, pastor, but she said to tell you that first, she does not e-mail men because her father, a retired U.S. Air Force colonel, told her that was not a good practice and definitely not the method to use to meet "Mr. Right." She also asked that you please understand she is old fashioned, and she would not call you because, in her Christian upbringing, men are supposed to call the ladies not vice versa!"

As he handed me Sandy Montgomery's business card, I looked it over and said, "Wow! You know, my dear friend Brother Ronnie, she has some 'spunk' doesn't she! Can you relay one more message to her?" He responded with a gleam in his eyes, "What would that request be?"

"If you happen to go back over that way, tell her, of course she is exactly right on both counts, and I am guilty on both! Tell her that I will call her today to become acquainted as soon as I get a chance." I was absolutely pleased that she was an "old-fashioned" lady who was right in honoring her father's wishes and not e-mailing or calling men. It was also refreshing to know that a real lady like this still existed in the world.

Divine Connection of Prophetic Fulfillment

I barely waited until he had left the parking lot before I fumbled around and found the card again. I quickly dialed the number to Ms. Sandy Montgomery's office. She could not talk very long because she had an office full of clients, but every single second we shared was totally anointed. She would finish my sentences in Scripture and I would finish hers in the same way. Everything we said was straight from the Word of God!

She had one of the most successful educational tutoring businesses in the region. Although we were both busy, we were excited about the possibility of a new godly friendship. Things were about to look up! I could tell by the amazing way God used this first conversation to spark my enthusiasm and excitement for life.

After I hung up, I sat back in my desk chair to begin writing, and the Lord reminded me that this day was the evening of the *third day of the prophecy!* I almost fell out of the chair, and I then jumped up and did a backward summersault on the carpet! The Atlanta prophet's word was true! Sandy was already so encouraging and I knew something was really extraordinary about her.

That night I tried calling her over and over again—at least 20 times—but I was only able to leave messages. Hopeful and determined to reach her, I dialed the number once more. This time I finally reached Sandy, who had just awakened from a deep, peaceful sleep the Lord had given her. Our conversations made me want more than anything to see her. However, Sandy said that during her sleep, God spoke to her, telling her to wait two weeks before meeting me in person.

We talked for hours, but it seemed as if only minutes passed because the conversations continued to be anointed by God. I told her I would call her again the next day and later tomorrow evening. As busy as I was, I found myself wanting to talk to her over and over again and looked forward to our daily conversations.

Then as our schedules allowed, we talked more frequently and I realized that the prophetic word was coming to pass—God was working miracles in my heart and life. During this time I was speaking words for the Lord into lives as I ministered all over the country. Now, I was actually living in an on-going prophetically directed adventure into real love and restoration. It was almost more than my heart could handle. I was living in a constant state of excitement finally meeting and seeing the "true love" of my life and God's answer to my dreams.

We got to know each other very well through our incredibly anointed long and frequent conversations. Soon I found myself wanting to marry this lady, and one night, I mustered the courage to ask her to marry me—right over the phone! She said she would rather wait on God's timing, but knew God was orchestrating a beautiful symphony of love in our hearts. Since she was only temporarily refusing my proposal, I felt the hand of God moving things swiftly to bring us together. I could hardly wait but knew Sandy was listening and hearing the Lord.

Weeks passed by quickly as we grew closer and closer through talks over the phone. We were amazed at how perfect we were for each other; God had prepared Sandy for me and me for Sandy. We were so much alike. With such an encourager and close friend, I no longer felt the sting of rejection. Many of you can identify with that last statement, because you know the pain of having your dreams destroyed and hopes shattered by the enemy or your own fatal wrong decisions. All we want is to be loved and to love without fear of losing it all again.

Yes, that is what I wanted most: *love, acceptance, and forgiveness—unconditional love!* I wanted to be *"accepted in the beloved"* in that type of intimate ministry that Jesus displayed. Jesus Christ totally devoted His personal ministry of love on earth in the world's first church model. Christ taught by mentoring a close-knit group He handpicked and called His disciples. He knew they would make mistakes. He knew they would vacillate and question Him. For the very first time, Jesus showed them and everyone, true love on earth. Jesus showed true love by ripping open and exposing religious lifestyles—and teaching compassion and mercy. In the beginning, Jesus' disciples did not completely understand His love, yet later all but one willingly either died or was persecuted to near death for the love of Jesus.

After losing so many things that were precious to me, I could understand the disciples' wariness about unconditional love. To protect my heart from additional hurt, I allowed my heart to be walled up by my own defense mechanisms—to stave off hopes and dreams, let alone feelings of ever knowing *true love*. At this checkpoint on the path, it seemed that I was right in the middle of this "true love on earth" feeling of completion. My heart was so full of love for Jesus—and for the lady He so lovingly sent to me—that there were times I would almost lose my breath. I would often tell Sandy, "You just made my heart stop, and I wish this moment in time would last forever. Oh Sandy, you 'respirate' me!"

Most of us do not realize it when we are going through tough times, but afterward, as God delivers us victoriously from the situation, we understand the reason for the bumps in our paths, or the course corrections. When we feel the cleansing water from the streams of life that only He can shower down on us, then we know His true love. Eventually everyone reaches a point when we cry out to God and say, "Lord, this is all of me. This is all that is left—shattered and abandoned hopes and dreams and a calling that has never been fulfilled. Please help me, Lord. Please make something worthwhile out of my life— help me be an offering to others."

Get ready, because He will answer the ones who are desperate for Him! *God is love*, waiting for us to say "Yes!"

Father's Example

Almighty God is the only example we have of true love—true unconditional love. He sent His son in the form of *Love* for His creation through Jesus Christ, our Redeemer. Jesus Christ of Nazareth is the *only* Savior of the world. He gave us His unconditional love by His total obedience to His Father God's plan— even to death on a cross. Jesus said, *"This is My commandment, that you love one another as I have loved you. Greater love has no one than this, than to lay down one's life for his friends"* (John 15:12,13 NKJV).

Jesus was the answer to the Lord's desire to close the gap between Heaven and earth and bring us to reconciliation with Himself. *"But small is the gate and narrow the road that leads to life,* **and only a few find it"** (Matt. 7:14 NIV, emphasis added). When I remember conversations I have had with hundreds of others looking for His love along the path, it is obvious that many have not found the true love they hunger to experience.

Living within the Kingdom of God is where we can dwell, reconciled with the love of the Father through the sacrificial offering of His only Son, Jesus Christ. Discovering the *true love of God is* the ultimate goal in life on earth. As we sojourn on this toll road to find God and His real love, we pay a price when we take the wrong exit. Will we settle for second best and make a hasty exit when the going gets rough or the storms get treacherous? After realizing our mistakes, we think getting back on the road will be easy; but, because it is a toll road, the cost for every mile will be levied. What you are willing to pay to find His heart is the amount it will cost. How much do you want to find true love?

FATHER'S HOPE CALLS YOU

Finding the genuine love of the Father and knowing real acceptance of being in His beloved family of fulfillment will destroy your insecurities. As you lay your head down for restful sleep at night, you will no longer worry about what people say or think about you—you will be focused on His heart and His thoughts.

Keep going my friends; your journey to becoming could be compared to a trip with an exciting friend who is accompanying you in the process of your destiny to Him. Resting at a roadside park is not leaving the journey; it provides a necessary time of respite during your lifelong expedition. Take a break and absorb the smells and views along the way. Do not be surprised that while you take a seasonal stop and enjoy the fresh new climate and His beauty of nature, the Father will visit with you and share valuable instructions for the road ahead. Listen for the Lord's voice calling you further into His presence. You will be inspired to continue, and I hope you find the true love of your life as I have found mine. The love is waiting just around the corner for you on your path to complete submission to God's will and surrender to His call and Word.

CHAPTER 8

New Beginnings
A True Love Story From Heaven

HEAR GOD'S VOICE AND OBEY

Many people ask me how I became so blessed and I quickly tell them that I did a lot of dying along the journey of the process. The second thing I tell them is that Sandy, my true love of my life and ministry partner, has been a pure source of blessing—she stood with me when no one else offered me a prayer. Our relationship has been a miracle of love that has given us both the strength and completeness that the Lord wanted for us. In the beginning there were negative voices prompted by an agitated religious spirit aimed at disarming our love, but God's mission prevailed. Nothing could ever separate this true love God Himself ordained and planned for our lives. Love takes on many assignments, and I am so thankful Sandy is the one called by God to love me.

The religious disorder never stops God's love and His voice—it only adds fuel to the destiny that God ordained before the foundations of the world. Nothing really ever disqualifies a person for the service of the King of kings. Even though throughout our entire relationship we were both following God's instructions explicitly—not even wanting to chance the possibility of "messing up"—God never ceased performing miracles daily to quicken our relationship so as to accomplish His will.

Sandy and I grew much stronger in our relationship with Him because we stayed, we prayed, we forgave, we gave, we searched for God's not man's direction, and we accepted the fact that there would always be more to do for Him than we could accomplish in a *lifetime*. I always liked that word lifetime; it has a nice ring to it.

God is amazing when He moves you—which is often quite suddenly! But the reality is that during our lifetime of service with the King, there will always be the religious spirit. We must learn to use it to our advantage to push us further into God's destiny. How could that be possible? It is possible because it brings to the surface areas or issues you need to face, so you can choose to die to them—die to your flesh and the world. When you simply fall on your face and surrender totally to Him, then your love for those who have hurt you becomes genuine. My love for them certainly was and will continue to be unconditional. Actually, I can see now how God used those hurtful things to bring me to my destiny. Only through the love of God can you love those who wanted to destroy you, and even love those you will never meet.

It is disheartening to see the game of church being played across our great nation. It is hard to accept the competition of polling church leadership over the next voice that God raises up. What happened to godly leaders' prayer closets, discernment, and producing fruit? Let God be the judge and allow Him to talk to His leaders.

I have, for the record, thrown out the advice of the Sanhedrin councils of churches, which includes leaders' blackball books, green room approval lists, blue books of bad blunders, red carpet lists for the upper echelon, and anything that promotes the worship of man rather than God Almighty. In this troubled world and age, we should not divert God's chosen vessels from bringing a fresh voice, a now word, and new approach.

This is nothing new to God. When Jesus walked on the earth, people who heard His voice also had a choice whether to obey—or not. From Wall Street to Main Street, all people have to make choices. Every one of our choices brings consequences—good or bad. Those of us on the road to God's destiny for us have the Bible as our guide. Even so, we will have deep down issues to deal with. I have made many mistakes in my life that I would rather put in the shredder and have them expunged, but they have helped shape who I am now, and where I am now. God makes a way. I cannot let past mistakes be deterrents for me to live to God's fullest plan in the here and now and future eternity with the King of kings and Lord of lords.

It is time to grow spiritual backbones. Do not be intimidated because you have not achieved a certain spiritual level assigned by self-appointed spiritual governors in a given amount of time, thus pleasing them. God does not care about how many people attend certain churches—He cares about you, me, each of His children. Large membership numbers are not indicators of God's anointing. God wants us to grow the Kingdom of God, not man's kingdom. Plain and simple, if we bow to other people's advice for our destiny fulfillment for His Kingdom, our path is subject to error. We are called by God and not by man. We are first and foremost accountable to God.

Love-based Not Fear-based

I feel the need to clarify once again the misguided teaching that stems from a fear-based doctrine that actually leads to "self and ministry council network preservation by fear tactics." There is a genuine belief by some church leaders today that humans, other than themselves, cannot correctly hear from God and obey His voice.

If apostles and prophets are the true foundation of the church, then why are some church leaders shaking in their shoes or floundering around, hoping the prophets will not cause a disturbance in the established order of their church?

If apostles and prophets are the foundation of the church, those who are on top of foundation and should feel secure in the love released from the fivefold ministry leadership foundation to do the work of the ministry. Citizens of His Kingdom will never feel free to launch out and do God's will if they are always concerned that a ruling elder will have a club of spiritual control waiting to beat down any contrary move. God has more for His citizens than church games that hold people as pawns in a maze of power.

The game is vibrant and being played all across this land today, but it will be ending soon, and many players will be realigning themselves to know the heart of the Father. Our Father is returning His heart to His own people, His sons and daughters. I pray that godly leaders will weigh and consider their actions. I pray that the trusted leaders will begin to repent that they became prey to a controlling spirit for base building and financial protections.

Yesterday's sheep and flocks saw many hides ripped off in front of them that they fled, splattered with blood, and often chose to meet in homes. This might be an option again, especially if we use genuine love, acceptance, and forgiveness as a base for demonstrating the greatness and love of the Father's heart! Home church may become more and more popular.

I certainly pray that leaders will surrender their control, repent of their fear-based attitudes that are borderline jealously motivated and religious spirited, and let the healing process begin. When George Barna discovered why a majority of people are not attending "formal church" any longer, most formal church leaders scoffed at the results.[1] Many leaders simply did not take this report seriously and wrote it off as another "trick of the devil" (he is given credit when we'd rather escape the slap of truth that is spiritual pride). They rebuked the "home church movement" as latent, or even open displays of rebellion. Oh, really? Isn't this similar to the day their movement shifted them into becoming the revolutionary?

This done-it-all-wrong-myself-once voice for God has learned a lot on the crazy (and very interesting) path of becoming a prophet. Will we one day finally understand this adventure of love when He calls us closer to His heart? That is left to the one in pursuit of the Father's love. That question should make any leader in the Kingdom of God fall on his face and seek the Lord God's heart! God is knocking on the door of our hearts now more than ever. He is surely seeking us more than we are seeking Him. We must change that scenario—we must become pursuers of God. We must become like my friend, Tommy Tenney, a "God Chaser!"

The Father is desperate for us to be servers of the Bread of Life, Jesus, for the hungry, the hurting, those in the middle of human wreckage. Are we willing to share His love, acceptance, and forgiveness for all humanity—*no matter what?*

THIRD TIME THE CHARM

After just a day of thinking about what had happened on "banishment day," I had planned to either drive to Mexico to minister and help complete a new church there or wait on what God would say to Sandy, hoping He would speak to her as He always did and give her the peace and assurance I had about getting married right away. Together, Sandy and I prayed earnestly about how God was redirecting my steps in ministry. I fasted and prayed to know the will of God. We experienced so many signs and many words from God. Also, while I traveling to different cities while ministering, we had absolutely astounding simultaneous dreams on the same nights, confirming that we were hearing from God implicitly and completely yielding to His will.

Sandy asked if I was dedicated to serving the Lord in ministry and to doing His calling in my life until Jesus came, or we went to be with Him. I said "Yes." This question was extremely important to her since she witnessed the extreme devastation I had just been through. I had a mandate that was non-negotiable for me to be His voice to the nations after having had the boardroom instruction presented in Heaven by my brother as a messenger of God. I would never detour from God's assignment!

Sandy told me that she had "prayed and weighed" the situation out before God that and she knew without question that God had orchestrated everything—even those things that seemed "not of God"—to have His will done to use us together as a ministry team.

She said that God told her after waiting for more than 10 years to remarry, that when the man He sent to her came along, he would be all that God had promised. "I'm letting you know I'm available to you and I love you John Mark Pool," Sandy said. "And," she continued, "there is no longer a need to wait the five to seven years we promised to wait, since you've you have been released from the church. I accept your previous proposal of marriage!"

I caught my breath and sighed and said, "Yes, I know you understand and I know you want this more than anything too—we will be a ministry team, and where God leads and what God says, we will do for the rest of our lives!"

"That is a promise from my heart to yours and God's!" she said.

I made sure her father approved of the marriage, and in addition, I suggested we have papers drawn up to protect her property and possessions. I had a farm in Texas and a few other assets, but I wanted her to know that my heart needed love, not her possessions. I had many experiences over the years, but never before had I encountered this kind of feeling about real true love. I had never really known love before—until Sandy.

We ordered flowers and made arrangements to meet with the preacher, as we wanted everything perfect for our wedding. We had all the paperwork signed, and the approvals and confirmations fell into place like clockwork. Just as God said, we were married under the large pecan tree on July 14, 2002, a beautiful Sunday afternoon, just five days following "banishment day."

Sandy looked like an angel in a dream come true, as she seemed to float up the garden steps into my arms that day. I had never felt such peace and happiness knowing I was in God's perfect will. God had reorchestrated what the enemy meant for harm, to launch me back onto the road leading to my greatest blessings. God gave us what we had both been dying to receive.

Sandy is the wife I have dreamed of all my life. She is also my God-called true love. As my spiritual ministry partner, she helps me in every aspect of life. When you get the "God choice" over a good choice, you have your dreams come true! Mine is with me 100 percent of the time on everything. We have learned the value of God's plan for us to back each other with love and prayer.

First we ask God and then we also consult each other prior to making decisions. Sandy has great discernment and this has become an invaluable gift in our marriage. Now Sandy and I hear from God together. We are alike in every way—we're on the same wavelength. We have actually simultaneously dreamed the very same dream; and when we review our dreams, we are so amazed at God. He has allowed us to have dreams that are spiritually illuminating to the point of giving specific instructions and warnings.

We are now in our fifth glorious and blessed year of marriage. I did not allow myself to imagine that from death, destruction, and devastation, God would provide abundantly more than I had known before. God gave Sandy and me a real, unconditional true love from Heaven. We want the best for each other; we share a friendship and undying true love that is incomparable. We enjoy ministry together that is proof of the unconditional love of the Father for His own. Many teach that divorce cancels your future, but we have learned that when the hurts happen; God's healing takes place and it may be the very moment to begin your future!

BECOMING HIS

God is not interested in man's idea of qualifications; He is looking for people of all walks of life who will simply dare to love Him and love others as themselves. When we share His love with others, He does not look to see if our credentials are in order, our plaques are on the wall, and that the community leaders all sanction our every move. No, God looks to see if our heart of love will fill in a gap and make up a hedge! He is looking for loving people who really care about a hurting world. We do not have to be licensed to win souls and change nations!

Although Sandy and I are ordained ministers and can legally marry others and perform ministerial rites and functions, those functions are not our ministry goals. We will do God's will whether or not we receive man's credentials. Our commitment to God and to each other is with our hearts for His. When you get to the point when you have weathered enough storms, and all you want to do is what the Father asks, then you are on the right path in the process of becoming.

Simply yield the right-of-way to the Father on your journey, and at the end of the process, you will be found with His entire beloved, laying their crowns down at His feet. What an awesome privilege it is to serve the King of kings and Lord of lords. When you are secure in the Father's love, the true love of your life, nothing else can by any means harm or stop you. No amount of money, fame, position, or earthly possessions can compare to that security and peace of mind. When we die to our plans and accept the Father's hand, everything changes.

Love on Him; and know that during your process of becoming, even when others hurt you, you must love them back and bless them as the Father does all of us. In His love, acceptance, and forgiveness He will remain with us forever. The Father is for you and He will complete your destiny as you give all of yourself to receive all of Him.

My prayer is that on this journey you will abide in His love, acceptance, and forgiveness forever. Be blessed on your path with all my love of the Father to you and your destiny.

ENDNOTE

1. "Americans Have Commitment Issues, New Survey Shows," George Barna report, 2006. http://www.barna.org/FlexPage.aspx?Page=BarnaUp-dateNarrow&BarnaUpdateID=235.

John Mark Pool Ministry

John Mark teaches the Prophetic Training Schools in many locations each year across the USA and to the Nations!

John Mark teaching
on TV programs
_____

John Mark teaching in a
BARN-Ark of Safety
in Vincennes IN.
_____

John Mark is known for
fiery & anointed preaching.

Many fellowships meeting
in shopping centers!
_____

John Mark & Sandy Pool
ministering God's Word
at Prophetic Conferences,
Crusades, Churches,
as well as Teach the
Apostolic/Prophetic
training schools in USA
and the Nations.

For scheduling:

www.wordtotheworldministries.org

WORD TO THE WORLD MINISTRIES

P. O. BOX 879 - BAKER, LA 70704

PHONE (225) 771-1774

Additional copies of this book and other
book titles from DESTINY IMAGE are
available at your local bookstore.

Call toll-free: 1-800-722-6774.

Send a request for a catalog to:

Destiny Image® Publishers, Inc.
P.O. Box 310
Shippensburg, PA 17257-0310

*"Speaking to the Purposes of God for This
Generation and for the Generations to Come"*

For a complete list of our titles,
visit us at www.destinyimage.com